THE WINNING HABIT

THE WINNING HABIT

How Your Personality
Makes You a Winner
or a Loser
in the Stock Market

by MARK J. APPLEMAN

The McCall Publishing Company

NEW YORK

Published simultaneously in Canada by
Doubleday Canada Ltd., Toronto

Library of Congress Catalog Card Number: 71–122112

SBN 8415–0031–2

The McCall Publishing Company
230 Park Avenue, New York, N.Y. 10017

Printed in the United States of America

For Marguerite,
who has always been a winner

Acknowledgments

This book owes much to many, only a handful of whom can be given their proper due in the appropriate place. For obvious reasons, none of the men and women who have involuntarily lent their "investor personalities" as object lessons will be identified. But I would like to express here my appreciation to a special few without whose aid, counsel or comfort the pages might still be blank.

When it began to appear to me—after six or seven years of filing away notes to myself in a folder marked WINNERS AND LOSERS—that success or failure in the stock market resulted in significant degree from investor habits that could be anticipated, I was far from utterly convinced. Was it just a personal slant or a really valid conclusion? And if valid, could the idea be developed into a useful book? For objective answers, I turned to the two most authoritative men of my acquaintance on Wall Street, Edmond duPont and Charles Moran, Jr. For their immediate and continued encouragement I was and am deeply indebted. At the outset also I sought the opinion of Everett Mattlin, a financial editor and writer whose judgment I respected, and he not only responded affirmatively but also took it upon himself to prod me along and root the book home.

Since no one individual—not this one anyway— knows all the facets of the securities business, let alone all the wrinkles of the investor mentality, it was frequently necessary to borrow from the wisdom and experience of others. Three who gave most generously of their time and knowledge were Lee J. Rand, Harold A. Rousselot and Llewellyn P. Young.

I was lucky too in having access to a pair of cooperative magicians. David Grace could always make his computers cough up in a matter of minutes or even seconds data that might otherwise have taken weeks to dig up and figure out, while John Greeley, equally resourceful, consulted his charts for me and filled in technical gaps.

After it was all down on paper—theory, people, statistical backup and interpretations—what was the sum total? I didn't know, my perspective having fuzzed in the writing. It was a great comfort therefore when Edwin B. Peterson, a tower of strength in the investment community, reviewed the manuscript and gave me the benefit of his suggestions.

And lastly, for personifying those rare virtues of patience, cheerfulness and commitment while typing and retyping from my unreadable longhand, my warmest thanks to Mrs. Willa-Jeanne Cennamo.

Whatever merit this book may have reflects in large measure the assistance and encouragement received from friends, partners and associates. Whatever deficiencies you may discover, errors of fact or misinterpretations, can be charged to no one but me.

Mark J. Appleman

Contents

THE WINNING HABIT

Introduction

This is a book about investors, not about investing.

For a lot of good reasons.

The country clubs are filled with successful investors who know nothing about the workings of the stock market, and care less. At the same time, Wall Street brokers can name you quite a few economists, professors of corporate finance, Wharton School graduates and chartered financial analysts, all estimable fellows, who have read most of the books on money management, and written a few themselves, but who can't make a right decision at the right time often enough.

As long as market information, theory and technique are available for the asking or for a modest fee, it's a wise investor who knows himself.

While a nice thing to have, a financial education is in itself no open door to investment success, any more than thorough familiarity with a driving manual gives a motorist the alertness, judgment, co-ordination and nerve with which to get through heavy traffic. Or, as the managing partner of one of the leading brokerage houses expressed it, "If you put all the drivers in Sherman tanks, they would still have accidents. It's the driver, not the car." Just so: it's the investor, not the investment vehicle.

What will make you successful—or unsuccessful—in

the stock market? In the final analysis, your qualities of judgment, temperament, courage, instinct and perseverence; your ability to differentiate between what you need and what you want out of your investment program; and, most important of all, except luck, the acuity of your insight into yourself. For you cannot expect suddenly to change your way of thinking and feeling and acting just at the moment you are called upon to decide whether to buy or sell a stock.

If, for instance, you are accustomed to weighing all of the relevant facts in arriving at your business or professional decisions, you are apt to follow the same approach with your investments.

If you are courageous (or timid) about substantial financial commitments of any kind, chances are you will be just as courageous (or timid) about committing yourself to your stockbroker.

If you tend to be trusting, you are likely to believe what you are told about an investment opportunity, especially if the source is reliable. If you tend to be cynical, you will probably discount what you hear regardless of the source.

If you have a history of emotional spasms about big decisions, you may be sorely tempted to plunge in fast, just to get it over with, and once in, you may be sluggish about getting out.

If you are very dependent on the good opinion of friends and associates, you may find yourself selecting stocks or bonds or mutual funds to meet the approval of others rather than your own investment objectives.

If you habitually back the favorite in sports events, you may like the current stock market favorites; and if you usually back the underdog at the stadium, you may have a predilection for securities that have not yet gained popular support in the market.

If you are prone to be bargain-conscious, you may be attracted to price before value in stocks.

The point is, if you're old enough to have a brokerage account, your personality is formed, your habits are set, your life style is pretty well established. You cannot expect your character to undergo a radical transformation at the sound of your stockbroker's voice on the telephone.

A very rich young stockbroker I know says that he can tell in a matter of minutes, before the first transaction is broached, whether a new client will turn out to be an investor or a speculator, a long-term holder or an in-and-out trader. He can also predict, he says, in the very first interview, whether the new client will be a success or a failure. Since that's how this particular stockbroker became so rich so young, I have to believe him. Besides, it's not really so difficult when you stop to think about it.

What are the telltale signs? First of all, whether and how you define your investment objective. Just saying, "I want to make money," doesn't count. Almost everybody says that (nobody has ever said, "I want *not* to make money in the market"), whether they mean it or not.

The poser is: How much money and how fast? How much risk can you afford to take, emotionally as well as financially? And do you have the courage—or the patience—to carry on to your goal? Do you think you have the knowledge and the time and the judgment to develop your own ideas—or will you be relying on recommendations from your broker or your investment adviser? And when you receive a recommendation, will you act at once on faith or impulse, or will you demand more facts and more time to deliberate? And just what kind of stocks do you cotton to—the glamors, the blue chips, the low-priced long shots over-the-counter, or what?

When your mind is made up, do you go all the way right away, or do you start out by getting your little toe wet and then easing your way in?

If your stock should rise a few points, will you call your broker to sell or to buy more? And, conversely, if your stock should drop a few points, will you phone your broker to buy more or to sell? In other words, can you live with your own objectives and your own judgments—in the absence of any material change in the facts—or will you get thrown by the first big dip or little bump in the market?

During the great bear market of 1969–70, did you sell out your holdings, switch to less vulnerable securities, or wait passively while your net worth dwindled away?

These are but a sampling of the early warning symptoms that can tell a bright broker—or you—that you are likely to turn out to be a big success or a little one, a modest loser or a financial basket case.

Success is a habit—so is failure. You form your success or failure habits early and you repeat them—unless by making the effort you change them!

But this is not to say, as some do, that there are winners and there are losers and never the twain shall meet. We all know successful businessmen who are flops as husbands or fathers or, indeed, as investors. And we also know successful investors who do not seem to be much good at anything else. What's more, the most successful investors make their share of market boo-boos, just as unsuccessful investors enjoy occasional profits.

In ten years of looking and listening on Wall Street I have never come across a system or formula that worked *for money* for anybody and everybody. Every single success I have seen or heard about has been individual. Every investor or speculator makes his own success or failure in his own way largely through the size and style of his own personality.

"Know thyself," saith Bias, Chilo, Cleobulus, Phemone, Plato, Pythagoras, Socrates, Thales (in alphabetical order) and the Delphic Oracle, according to *Bartlett's Familiar Quotations.*

Also saith Cervantes: "Make it thy business to know thyself, which is the most difficult lesson in the world."

Amen.

"If you don't know who you are," adds the contemporary "Adam Smith" in his brilliant and entertaining book *The Money Game,* "this [the stock market] is an expensive place to find out."

Yes, but . . .

It usually costs money to learn by experience, and in the stock market, as in many another worthwhile pursuit, you may not profit from the lesson until you pay for it. The trick, it seems to me, is to pay willingly as much as it's worth to you but no more if you can help it. Which means not only accepting such losses as cannot be avoided but also taking stock of the person who made the wrong decisions. And not merely for the discipline or perverse satisfaction of acknowledging *mea culpa* but primarily to overcome weakness and cultivate strength, to catch a sense of your own rhythm so that if you decide to dance you can keep in tune with the market.

One way to get to know yourself at minimum expense is through self-analysis, as Bernard Baruch attests.

Early in his career, writes Baruch in his autobiography, "I began a habit I was never to forsake—of analyzing my losses to determine where I had made my mistakes. This was a practice I was to develop ever more systematically as my operations grew in size. After each major undertaking—and particularly when things turned sour—I would shake loose from Wall Street and go off to some quiet place where I could review what I had done and where I had gone wrong. At such times I never sought to excuse myself but was concerned solely with guarding against a repetition of the same error. . . . Periodic self-examination of this sort is something all of us need."

Through periodic self-examination Bernard Baruch made the stock market a most profitable place to find out who he was.

Another way, perhaps a little less difficult, to get to know yourself is by example, by identifying your personality or style in others.

It is the purpose of this book to help you do just that: to recognize your own weaknesses and strengths by observing and analyzing the habit patterns of other men and women with reference to their market decisions. For the decision, after all, is habit in action—all theory, technique, information, judgment and character unequivocally expressed as an order to buy, sell or hold.

Most of us try to look at ourselves occasionally, and some, the more determined among us, to improve on what we see. In the following pages you will be afforded an opportunity to see yourself as your stockbroker might see you, so that if you wish to change your luck you will have a pretty good idea of where to change yourself.

Here, then, is a kind of "investor's mirror" in book form, meant not only to reflect the way you look and act but also to guide you in the light of today, tomorrow or next year, whatever the mood of the market.

1

The
Market Masochists

How do you style yourself—as a winner? loser? or sometimes one, sometimes the other?

If your market achievements fall short of your objectives, would you account for your unwinning performance as voluntary or otherwise?

Are you sure?

Many a stockbroker has been baffled, at times offended, by a client's apparent will to lose. In the boardroom, each new day presents a modern adaptation of Dostoevski or Tolstoi, featuring at least one character with a dark, tormented soul who goes out of his way to take on great dollops of pain and suffering. Ordinarily sensible, commissions-paying citizens strip themselves of their savings with a persistence reminiscent of ancient kings and queens in a Greek tragedy, hell-bent on their own destruction.

But the general impression is otherwise. Even in an age fraught with Freud it is taken for granted that no one buys securities except to make money. Some seem to feel that since Freud's observations on masochism were drawn from a variety of kooks in Vienna around the turn of the century, and since his reference was specifically sexual, the only relevance is to a handful of mixed-up Austrians whose libidos have long since ceased to trouble them.

The will to lose has been universalized and made all-purpose only in the last few decades. In 1941, in his book *Masochism in Modern Man*, Dr. Theodor Reik promulgated the theory of "social" masochism. No longer confined to sex or religion, to whips and spurs or hair shirts and fasting, the new everyman's masochism embraces all levels and forms of society, neatly summed up by Reik in three words, "victory through defeat."

Still, even if some of us are willing to concede that there may be (other) people who wish to punish themselves for sins, real or fancied, or to expiate infantile guilt feelings by being beaten or impoverished, the question remains, why would they do it in the stock market, which is supposed to be a trading center for securities? Doesn't the idea of masochism in the market smack of rationalization, the Unorganized Parlor Shrinks of America trying to obfuscate the obvious— that stocks go down as well as up?

The question was put to our friendly neighborhood psychiatrist, whose patients include both investors and speculators. "One of the most difficult phenomena we have to cope with today," he said, "is the subconscious desire of many people to lose in the stock market, to pay back their gains from other sources. Paradoxically, they succeed in their subconscious desire to fail in their conscious aim."

Unlike psychoanalysts, psychiatrists and psychologists, the stockbroker meets his social masochists in action. And the conscientious broker is particularly pained by a will to fail, because it reflects on him, or so he feels. It is no consolation at all to know that the client who just dropped a bundle has thereby temporarily lifted from his heart a heavy feeling of guilt or alleviated the itch in his soul.

Here from the brokerage house view are glimpses of two men and a woman whose losing performances were so persistent and so much of a pattern as to suggest a ritual purpose or compulsion.

Victory Through Defeat?

Bob is a public relations executive, intelligent, practical, with a working knowledge of corporate finance and the securities industry. About ten years ago, when he was still in his twenties, Bob inherited over a hundred thousand dollars, which after careful study he invested in good quality, conservative stocks. In a rising market, he was doing above-average-well when and presumably was satisfied for a while, until suddenly he decided that he ought to do better faster. Liquidating his holdings one at a time, he began taking greater risks, seeking more aggressive performance. Although several of his gambles paid off nicely, just as many cost him heavily. The net result was a standoff. But instead of going back to his earlier style of conservative—and successful—investing, he started trading the volatile issues, like Xerox and Polaroid, on margin. In a couple of years Bob had squandered his entire inheritance.

When he found himself broke, Bob was badly shaken up. But being resourceful as well as intelligent, he immediately tried to analyze what he had done and why it had turned out so disastrously. Then he sat down and wrote a book about it, documenting his errors and pointing out just where he had gone wrong. The book made a strong case for long-term investing as opposed to in-and-out gambling, and sold well. Soon Bob's royalties from book sales, magazine rights and a book-club selection exceeded his losses in the market. And once again he was putting his money into stocks.

It would be nice to report that, having learned a costly lesson and preached it profitably, Bob now practiced it. But that isn't the case. What Bob did was to turn over his brokerage account—and full discretion—to a hot-shot trader, who took him down the same steep, speculative road as before, this time selling short volatile issues like Polaroid and Memorex. In a couple of years Bob hit zero again. But he felt better about it the second time, because he could blame the trader for the debacle.

Anybody can make a mistake, of course. But anybody who makes the same kind of mistake twice may be considered awfully foolish or careless. Bob is neither. Yet twice he has chosen to follow a foolhardy course.

One cheerful note: Any day now we can expect another of Bob's brilliantly analytical, solidly documented financial true-confessions that, hopefully, will earn him a third big stake with which to start the whole cycle all over again.

Beat or Be Beaten

Mike, general agent in the financial district for one of
the top three insurance companies, is a happy-go-lucky
bachelor in his fifties. A star football player in college,
Mike is still a rugged competitor on the squash courts
of the Downtown Athletic Club where he goes for a
sweat-up and convivial lunch just about every noon.

As far as money is concerned, Mike is fixed for life,
the hereafter too; and canny enough to have provided
for a lady he once thought of marrying but didn't,
through a charitable foundation set up initially to help
cope with his high tax bracket. As you might gather,
Mike is anything but a pushover or a patsy. He hates
to lose—and yet that is exactly what he keeps on doing
in the stock market.

Mike started dabbling in securities tentatively, as a
gesture of reciprocity toward a brokerage firm for which
he had written some insurance. But when he found that
the market offered all-seasons action and a chance to
score big every day of the working week, he jumped
in with both feet.

Even at first Mike couldn't be bothered with stocks
that might appreciate in value by 10 to 15 percent a
year with relatively moderate risk. Dividends and capital gains were "for the peasants," he said. What he was
after was "pizzazz." He wanted challenge and the glory
of knocking Wall Street for a loop. He scorned "spec-
tator stocks that you just sit and watch." When he went
into a game, he played to win—or so he said.

The stocks Mike chose to play with were those in the

news, the spectaculars. He especially enjoyed dazzling his buddies by his ability to get in on hot new issues. When unable to obtain shares of a scarce offering from one broker, he switched to another. His market performance, as a result, was a perpetual roller coaster, up and down. Mike pretended it was all a lot of laughs, and maybe it was, because he kept bouncing his brokers and buying more of the sizzly Fourth of July Roman-candle issues—with more of the same kind of fizzly results.

At last report Mike had booted away what was a great deal of money even for him and was going at it harder and heavier than ever before—playing catch-up ball, determined to beat the market or be beaten in the attempt.

Why didn't Mike quit when he found that he was a steady loser, or change his tactics? One possible answer is that he is a nonstop gambler. Another is that he is a masochist, which may be saying the same thing. If he wasn't enjoying his losses—and the opportunity to feel sorry for himself—all he had to do was get out of the market.

The Ehrenkranz Syndrome

Louis Ehrenkranz is a seasoned stockbroker. A one-time high school teacher of English, Louis broke into the securities business in Brooklyn, where he discovered a strain of sadomasochism that he regards as not so rare but special. Let Louis, a compassionate though incisive wit, tell you about it.

"Take Mrs. Farber, for instance. In the three years I

knew her she had eight other brokers plus one burial to her credit.

"Who is Mrs. Farber? A quiet (always quiet), unassuming, gray-haired lady in her sixties who moves with slow, careful dignity. Everything about her suggests that she has just finished making a delicious chicken soup for her appreciative family, and just happened to be passing by, so she is stopping in to ask her broker a question. Her plain black coat and unfrivolous hat, and her quiet (always quiet) voice attests to the fact that she is humble, yea, even ignorant, when it comes to the market. Indeed, she is that sweet old mother of us all asking for help in a world of ferocious wolves.

"Now Mrs. Farber is sitting beside me, speaking in a voice so low I can hardly hear her. And all the time, as I am straining for her words and trying to keep my voice as low as hers, she is smiling at me benignly. But don't be deceived as I was, please. Let me take you into my confidence. Mrs. Farber was deliberately trying to drive herself into the poor house and me into a frenzy from which I could not (she hoped) recover. If she'd had her way, my last days would be spent on a funny farm hearing the whispering voice of a sweetly smiling, gray-haired grandmother on welfare. You think I'm mad—suffering from delusions? Here's a sample of this old gal's style on a Monday—any Monday—morning. But please remember, at no time does *she* raise her voice.

MRS. F. Good morning, Louie.
L. E. Good morning, Mrs. Farber.
MRS. F. [*Shyly*] What do you think of Ronson Corp?
L. E. I beg your pardon?

MRS. F.   I asked, what do you think of Ronson Corp?

L. E.   Not very much, Mrs. Farber, not for you.

MRS. F.   [*Slowly nodding her head in agreement*] Buy me 100 shares, Louie.

L. E.   You didn't understand me, Mrs. Farber.

MRS. F.   [*Still quietly, almost absent-mindedly, in fact*] Who says?

L. E.   I said I didn't like it. Not now. And not for you. [*A long, long pause like a break in a communications circuit*] You see, Mrs. Farber, appliance makers are working at full capacity, and the company will be hard put to equal last year's earnings. Also, the stock has no major sponsorship.

MRS. F.   God knows you're right.

L. E.   [*Sighs with relief*]

MRS. F.   Buy me 100 shares now.

COMES TUESDAY

MRS. F.   Louie, what do you think of Jerrold Electric?

L. E.   [*In an effort to be more forceful this time*] I think it's junk.

MRS. F.   You don't like it?

L. E.   It's junk. [*With a second effort*] Garbage.

MRS. F.   I know.

L. E.   Good.

MRS. F.   Should I buy some?

L. E.   No! NO!

MRS. F.   [*More quietly even than usual*] Please, Louie, don't yell.

L. E.   I'm sorry, Mrs. Farber. I just don't want you to make a mistake.

MRS. F.   [*Smiling gently*] Buy me 100 shares of Jerrold Electric.

COMES WEDNESDAY

"I arrive at the office with a fresh idea. I am not going to give Mrs. Farber a chance to agree with me and then do just the opposite of what I recommend. I am going to fox her by acquiescing immediately to any purchase suggestion she might make. Hopefully, she will be so flummoxed by my concurrence that she will change her mind. So today Jerrold Electric is going to be the best stock on the board, if she asks about it. Ronson is going to be an excellent choice, if she broaches it in that shy, quiet voice. I am absolutely not going to wind up yelling today. I am going to agree with Mrs. Farber instantaneously. Today a sane new world will be born. Get ready. Here she comes in all her unassuming delicious-chicken-soup dignity.

MRS. F.　Good morning, Louie.

L. E.　Good morning, Mrs. Farber.

MRS. F.　What do you think of Maxson Industries?

L. E.　[*Not sure he has heard correctly*] Terrific.

MRS. F.　[*Too polite to show emotion*] And what do you think of Vendo?

L. E.　Good. Very good.

MRS. F.　[*After a longer pause than usual*] Louie . . . ?

L. E.　Yes, Mrs. Farber?

MRS. F.　[*The old gentle smile playing on her lips*] What do you think of Ronson?

L. E.　An outstanding investment.

MRS. F.　And what do you think of Jerrold Electric?

L. E.　I like it very, very much.

MRS. F.　Louie?

L. E.　Yes, Mrs. Farber?

MRS. F.   Sell 100 Ronson and 100 Jerrold.

L. E.   What?

MRS. F.   Sell my Jerrold and Ronson.

L. E.   [*Outmaneuvered but still fighting*] What are you saying?

MRS. F.   I was thinking last night. Ronson is operating at full capacity and doesn't seem to have any sponsorship. Jerrold looks like garbage to me. Please sell.

L. E.   [*Suddenly screaming*] Then why did you buy it? Why did you spend the money?

MRS. F.   [*Almost inaudible*] I don't get the right advice from you.

L. E.   WHAT?

MRS. F.   You shouldn't have let me buy that junk. You should sit me down quietly and say, "Mrs. Farber, this is no good. This isn't for you." Instead, you yell. It's not right, Louie. It's not right. You should help me. After all, I depend on you. [*With a quiet air of finality*] Sell it, and next time try to give me good advice.

COMES THURSDAY

"If April is the cruelest month, then Thursday has got to be simply awful. Here comes quiet, ladylike Mrs. Farber with something new in her soup—arsenic, no doubt.

MRS. F.   Good morning, Louie.

L. E.   Good morning, Mrs. Farber.

MRS. F.   Louie, what do you think I ought to do?

L. E.   [*Unable to catch the words*] I beg your pardon?

MRS. F.   What do you think I ought to buy?

L. E.   [*With a new lease on life*] Rheingold. It's selling at 25½.

MRS. F.   You really think it's good? Confidentially?

L. E.   I think you ought to buy 200 shares.

MRS. F.   Do it.

L. E.   [*Triumphant*] Done!

COMES FRIDAY

"Had I only known then what I know today about the inhumanity of nice little old ladies to optimistic young men who are trying to help them, I would not have been so happy to see Mrs. Farber arrive and take the chair beside me.

MRS. F.   Louie, what do you really think about the Rheingold we bought yesterday?

L. E.   Don't sell it.

MRS. F.   Who said anything about selling?

L. E.   I like the stock.

MRS. F.   What?

L. E.   I like the stock. Nothing has changed since yesterday. They are still selling beer. [*Voice rising*] Don't sell it!

MRS. F.   Louie, I would like to sell 200 shares of Rheingold.

L. E.   No! Please!

MRS. F.   [*Very quietly*] Sell.

"Mrs. Farber sold Rheingold at 25⅞ that morning but my story doesn't end there. Five minutes later the stock began showing signs of strength. And when it appeared on the tape at 26½ Mrs. Farber came back to my desk. 'Louie,' she offered sweetly, 'I think I made a mistake.' I nodded sadly and we both watched the tape. Ten minutes later Rheingold was up to 27.

" 'Louie, I think we made a mistake.'

"The 'we' made me wince but I kept my silent vigil over the tape.

"When Rheingold hit 29⅝ later in the day, Mrs. Farber, who was still there, turned to me and said in a hushed, forgiving tone, 'Louie, you made a terrible mistake.'

" 'What do you mean,' I shouted, slamming my ashtray on my desk. '*We* made a mistake!'

" 'No, Louie,' she corrected me softly, 'I said *you* made a mistake. Don't, please, take me into a partner with your foolishness. And don't, please, ever high-pressure me again. Imagine, your selling my Rheingold. Such a good company . . .'

"At this, I'm afraid, I became incoherent and began waving my arms about, trying to right the record and at the same time get away from her.

"Turning to the crowd that was gathering around us, she said in her usual quiet voice but with a fresh touch of compassion, 'I don't hate Louie. I feel sorry for him. He's so nervous. Look at him, sputtering and waving like a windmill. Listen, it's none of my business. Maybe he doesn't get along with his wife. But why should he take it out on me? Don't ask what a week I put in with that nervous man. And now on Friday he sells my Rheingold just before it goes up. Must be something wrong with him.' "

Perhaps psychology doesn't explain everything but it does give us a lead.

Why was Mrs. Farber so consistently perverse? For the sadistic pleasure of embarrassing and discrediting her broker? For the masochistic pleasure of losing her money? Or both?

Investors who are self-punishers find ingenious ways to indulge themselves. Many, having sold a stock that subsequently rises, will refuse to buy it back no matter how rosy its prospects. Since one stock that goes up 10 points is just as rewarding as any other that goes up the same number of points, the investor who lays off a stock just because he once sold it is punishing himself for his previous "mistakes."

Some self-punishers will also try to chastise a stock. They act like children who punch a chair against which they have stubbed a toe. Having lost money in an issue or missed a rise by failing to follow a buy recommendation, they will then sell the stock short—seeking vengeance and vindication in the decline of the issue and also, perhaps, an opportunity to take another beating.

Although no one is right all the time and everyone must expect to lose money sometimes, without deep-down self-analysis, the habitual high-risk-taker is probably a market masochist. Since the short-term speculator doesn't know when to buy and the long-termer can't tell when to sell, both are virtually guaranteed a chance to lose, suffer and repent.

Why do they do it? They don't know and they don't seem to want to stop, even though the stock market is one of the more expensive places to practice self-flagellation. Perhaps the will to win and the will to lose, apparently emotion over mind, are not unlike those purely physical processes of anabolism and catabolism: Each of us existing in a state of tension between the drive to forge ahead and the urge to drop out; somewhere between the positive and negative poles we strike our balance and achieve an emotional metabolism.

Or, perhaps, as our friendly neighborhood psychiatrist puts it, "Habitual losers in the stock market are people who have not found the right outlet for their real purpose."

2

The
Tagalongs

The tagalongs are a numerous, gregarious clan who all like to go along for the ride, playing follow-the-leader. They do the same with their investments, birds of a feather flocking together for the sake of sweet sociability or some other benefit not directly connected with capital gain or dividend income. For the deep student of tagalongs the best observatories are in Florida, Southern California and other sunny resorts where lonesome senior citizens cluster in boardrooms like seven-sister bushes. Mrs. Piddlipom, an independent soul, decides to buy 300 Ampex. Word spreads instantly as the order is put in. By the time Mrs. Piddlipom's trade appears on the screen, a matter of minutes, there may be a half dozen more orders to buy Ampex. Perhaps Mrs. Piddlipom had sound reasons, but what about the

others? Do they respect her judgment or do they fear
that she might get ahead of them? Are they friends
eager to share a friend's luck or do they seek security in
sharing a commitment as a group?

The tendency to follow suit can be found whenever
two or more investors get together. One says, "After
Penn Central went bankrupt, I sold all my railroad
stocks." And if the other happens to be a tagalong who
owns railroad stocks, he may call his broker and, regardless of the latter's advice, dump the shares so as not to
be left behind to "face the music" alone.

You must know a dozen tagalongs who habitually
earn less and lose more. You may even be one yourself.
Let's take a look at three individuals and see if there is
a recognizable pattern in their market behavior.

Old Tagalong

Old Tagalong happens to be vice president in charge
of personnel for a major Wall Street house. Originally
an efficiency expert with a midtown company of management consultants, several years ago Old Tagalong
came downtown to make a study of personnel practices
for his present firm, and stayed on to implement the
policies he had recommended. A distinguished-looking,
elderly gentleman, Old Tagalong knows his job and
does it very well; but because he is still identified with
Uptown, he thinks of himself as an Outsider. He has
one not-so-secret ambition, to crack the Inner Circle
as a director or senior vice president, more as a sign of
acceptance than anything else. He would like to be able
to talk to the truly financial types of his firm—such as
the brokers and the traders, the research director and

the investment banking people—about their end of the business, as one of the boys. Since he is wealthy and close to retirement, his ambition is clearly more fraternal than material. Yet the only way open to him, he feels, to stake out a common ground with his associates is through his personal investments.

Old Tagalong, lunching with the over-the-counter trader, a vice president, will inquire casually, "Are you buying anything now for yourself?" Receiving some such reply as, "I'm putting away a little Christiana for the kids," Old Tagalong will promptly decide to buy Christiana for his grandchildren.

"What's the market doing this morning?" Old Tagalong might ask the research director at lunch. "Telephone's starting to get a little play from the institutions," could be the word. "I think I'll build up a position, too," Old Tagalong would say, throwing in his lot with the smart money managers.

Since the stocks he goes along with are usually top quality, his losses as a rule are modest, and Old Tagalong can regard them as an entertainment expense, like his luncheon club dues. Whatever it costs him, it buys what he wants most, a feeling of belonging, a sense of being on stage instead of backstage sorting out personnel.

Only once has Old Tagalong been known to protest the price of belated participation. From the vice president in charge of operations Old Tagalong had learned that his firm was installing new Control Data computers; and further, that the operations man, a seasoned Wall Streeter, had supported his product choice by buying Control Data stock at 38. No sooner was he back from lunch than Old Tagalong put in an order

to buy 100 Control Data at the market (by then 45),
thrilled not only to be going along with an important
associate but also to be endorsing his firm's good judgment. For almost a year afterward, with the greatest
satisfaction, Old Tagalong watched his Control Data
climb vigorously until it passed 100 (this was in 1964).
By now all of his firm's top officers knew that Old
Tagalong was "in" Control Data and they were greeting
him at lunch with, "Well, how's your highflier today?"

As happens to the best of stocks, Control Data eventually peaked out—at 109½—and started to slide. Old
Tagalong, still watching faithfully, never dreamed that
the public could be so fickle as to desert a company
that made such fine computers. When the stock touched
45, his purchase price, Old Tagalong put in an anxious
call to the operations director, only to learn that the
latter had sold *his* Control Data at least a year before,
at 106.

"Why didn't you tell me?" demanded Old Tagalong.

"You didn't ask me," replied the operations man.

Hating to be the only loser he knew in Control Data,
Old Tagalong decided to wait a little longer in the
hope that the stock would turn around and restore his
profit. From everything he'd read—and he was reading
quite a bit about Control Data these days—he could
see no reason why the issue should be in such a steep
decline. It was just that public confidence had faltered
or, to be more correct, had shifted elsewhere temporarily. But when the stock sagged to 42, Old Tagalong
joined the public, however reluctantly, and entered a
sell order.

He continued to watch the quotations, of course, out
of habit or sentiment, and as Control Data sank lower

and lower, his attitude changed. He became well satisfied with himself, because he had been wise enough to
bail out earlier.

After dropping below 25, however, Control Data
turned around and reversed its course rapidly until in
about nine months it was touching 100 once more. There
was a look of hurt in Old Tagalong's blue eyes. Then,
after an interval of backing and filling, Control Data
resumed its upward trend and, in under six months,
topped 150. That finished it for Old Tagalong. He
never bothered to look at Control Data again.

Miss Tagalong

While Old Tagalong might be able to chalk up his
modest losses and modest gains to the escalating cost
of business entertainment these days, a young lady in a
less enviable position is Miss Tagalong, let's call her, a
high-fashion model, very attractive, and sensible
enough to be thinking ahead to the day when she will
no longer be so young and so pretty and so much in
commercial demand.

Although she doesn't know a short from a long, and
numbers bore her, she is skipping along after her circle
of friends in the stock market. *Her* circle is made up
largely of fashion photographers, stylists, her agent,
and advertising art directors, young swingers for the
most part. And *their* bag is to go where the action is—
"yo-yo" stocks, "hot" new underwritings and thinly
held unlisted issues characterized by low price and high
volatility. "How much can you lose at $4 a share? And
if it goes to 20, you've quintupled your money." Or so
the argument goes.

Miss Tagalong would like to prepare a financial cushion for the future, but having neither the temperament nor the talent to lay out and follow an investment program, she relies on the tips of her friends. Somebody in her circle hears something somewhere chic and tells somebody else who sooner or later tells Miss Tagalong. As a result, she is rarely in at the beginning or out before the bitter end. At least twice in six years Miss Tagalong has ridden a roaring bull market in cheap unlisted issues from semi-boom to full bust. The last time she was wiped out, she remarked sadly, "It looked so really great for a while. *Every*thing was going up, then suddenly *poof!*" And when told that she should either stay out of the market or concentrate on quality stocks with low risk and good growth potential over the long pull, Miss Tagalong agreed. "Guess you're right," she said. "I promise if I ever have any money again, I'm going to put it into good, safe stocks." She won't, probably. As soon as the next tide of popular speculation comes in, as it does recurrently, Miss Tagalong may rationalize that *just because* she is now so much older she must go along with her friends who, in turn, may rationalize that being so much older, they must, at all costs, continue to identify with the younger, swinging, currently with-it fashion crowd.

Young Dr. Tagalong

Young Dr. Tagalong is a case of another sort about which you may make your own diagnosis and prognosis. The symptoms observed and reported follow:

Young Dr. Tagalong came into my life in a midtown restaurant where my wife and I were dining with friends. A stocky, pleasant-featured, balding young man, he approached our table and, greeting one of our friends, asked, "How's American Tobacco?"

"We just resigned the account," replied our friend, who is in the advertising business.

"I heard," said Young Dr. Tagalong. "That's why I'm asking. You had some stock. What are you doing about it now?"

"Sold it," was the reply.

"That's what I should do," nodded Young Dr. Tagalong, "sell mine, too."

At this point our mutual friend hastened to caution, "Look, Doc, I don't know anything about the stock. Only reason I sold mine is we gave up the account. It could be a real good deal for all I know. Why don't you ask him?" He pointed to me. "He's in Wall Street."

Since I didn't have a ready opinion on the stock, I promised to check our research analysts and to let the young man know what they thought. We exchanged cards and the next day when I phoned him at his office to relay the fundamental and technical opinions I had obtained, Young Dr. Tagalong was both grateful and gracious. "I'd like you to sell my tobacco and buy me whatever you're buying for yourself."

I tried to explain that brokering was not my end of the investment business, but he would not listen. "Look, all my patients and colleagues are making money in the market. Me, I'm a bum in the market. I don't mind the money, I can afford the money. I just hate to be the bum. When everybody's bragging about how well they're doing, what am I supposed to say? My colitis practice is up? Or my ulcer patients have split two for one? Or complain about my bleeding losses? It's not that I mind so much even the losing. I just hate to be the one idiot that's doing the losing while everybody else is raking in the profits. Call it ego, if you want, but it's a lousy feeling."

I offered to refer several able brokers to him so that he might choose one. "I won't be any trouble," he hung on. "I don't even want to know what you're buying or selling until after you do it. Just do for me whatever you're doing for your family. That'll be good enough for me. I trust you."

Sympathetic and doubtless flattered, I made the tactical mistake of inquiring about his investment objectives. "Money's not my object," he hastened to assure me. "I'm not in it for the money. I've got a good practice—more than I can handle—like you, I'll bet. I don't care whether it's long term or short term. I won't feel bad if I don't top anybody. Just so I'm not the only bum on Park Avenue. Pick me some stocks you like— as long as it's not widows' and orphans' stuff. I can't get much attention talking about Telephone or utilities."

Foolishly, I mentioned Standard Oil of California, a recommendation of our research department at that time. "Fine!" he exclaimed. "Buy me 100. I've been hearing a lot about the oils lately. Look, I've got about $150,000 worth of stock. I used to have more but I had these lousy brokers. I'll turn it all over to you. Now, what else besides Standard Oil of California?"

Only after we had been round and round several more times did I persuade him to meet with Paul, a young associate who had built up a loyal clientele (an important sign to me) with a steady, if not spectacular, track record. A few days later I learned from Paul that Young Dr. Tagalong had sold his tobacco and bought Socal. I assumed that all was now as it should be with Young Dr. Tagalong.

I was mistaken, of course. Within the month Young Dr. Tagalong was on the phone. "It must be me," he began. "Everything's down except the oil you gave me. I can't hold you responsible for the other fellow, but I believe you owe it to me to say whether it's me or it's him. If it's him, you've got to handle my account yourself or else I'm taking it to another brokerage house. I'm tired of having every broker in town make a bum out of me."

Paul had a different story to tell. After selling his tobacco and buying his oil, Young Dr. Tagalong asked for additional buy recommendations. Paul promised to send him current research reports to read. "Look, I don't want to waste my time on that stuff," Young Dr. Tagalong exclaimed. "Just tell me who's buying what." When advised that such information was confidential, Young Dr. Tagalong apologized, rephrasing his demand. "Look, who's your most successful client—I don't want his name. Get me? I'm not asking you to breach a professional confidence. Just tell me his stocks. I don't care who he is, just so he's a winner. Let me have his picks. When you don't know the road, I always say, let somebody drive who does."

With some misgivings, Paul was persuaded to list the holdings of his most successful account—without revealing the client's name, of course. He was then instructed as follows: "O.K., now, whatever this winner of yours buys, you buy it for me, get it? When he sells it, you sell it for me, too. O.K.?"

Paul made an effort to explain the obvious, that different people usually differed as to investment objectives and resources as well as temperament. To no avail. Young Dr. Tagalong insisted on jogging along after Paul's "winner."

Since nobody picks winners exclusively, and every stock, no matter how bright its prospects, fluctuates in response to a multitude of variable factors, the inevitable happened quite soon and Young Dr. Tagalong suffered fresh losses. "I read the financial pages," he complained to me over the phone. "When 692 stocks are up and 691 down, why should mine always be among the downs? How do I explain that to people without just saying, 'Look, I'm a bum'?"

Inasmuch as all the stocks he was holding appeared to be good values intrinsically, I prescribed the best remedy I knew in the circumstances: patience. But as one long accustomed to prescribing the same medicine, he was indignant. His account is now being handled by another broker, who, perhaps, will be able to help Young Dr. Tagalong achieve the non-bum status he seeks after office hours by providing him with an infallible model to follow.

To some extent, all of us on occasion become trailers, simply because we can't always be pacesetters and because there's usually somebody doing better than we are who can show us the way. The outcome depends on *which* crowd we're running after, and *where* they're headed. Bringing up the rear may be all right if it gets us "to the church on time." But we have all seen in recent years how the herd instinct can stampede both the bears and the bulls.

Old Tagalong had ample opportunity to double his money in Control Data, had he been seeking to make financial—instead of social—capital out of his investment. But there's no cause to feel sorry for him. Old Tagalong is getting his money's worth by way of luncheon conversation and a feeling of belonging to the inside world of the financial community.

Young Dr. Tagalong owned a portfolio of good-quality stocks that might have netted him a respectable profit had he held on to them until their potential was realized; but he didn't. He will probably continue to lose self-respect as well as money until he immunizes himself against the sheep virus, *me-too.* If he must match killings in the market, then he might consider limiting his risks by investing in triple-A-rated bonds, while dissembling to his patients and colleagues (as some of them may be doing to him) about being in on the current buzz stocks.

For Miss Tagalong there is neither consolation nor easy conversion. She has a real need to prepare a source of income and security for the now not-so-far-off future. She has good intentions of putting her spare cash into stocks with growth potential for the long pull, which in her case might be two to five years. And yet she is hooked. Skipping along with her kicky crowd, as she feels she must to keep working, she trades in nervous cats and dogs for which the long term is right now. When timing is all-important, a habit of being among the last ones in or out can have cruel consequences.

3

Plungers and Procrastinators

While plunging and procrastinating may be opposite reactions, they are also reciprocal symptoms of the same emotion: anxiety. Although the plunger's posture may appear more dashing, and the procrastinator may resemble a brooding hen as he waits for the decision to make itself, the difference is mainly one of style. Both are in doubt. In either case the emotional state rules—or over-rules—the investment objective. The plunger voids himself of his anxiety by taking action precipitately. The procrastinator, choking up, is incapable of acting at all. In neither case does the investor serve his self-interest except by coincidence.

Oddly enough, the compulsive plunger and the compulsive procrastinator may be the very same individual, under different degrees of stress. Any one person, you,

perhaps, may be a plunger at certain times, a procrastinator at others. Think about it. Haven't you ever
sat on a difficult decision too long? And haven't you
sometimes made your move prematurely, before giving
full consideration to the consequences? Which you
do when depends on the inner you, your tolerance
for stress, your response to the unknown (some draw
back in fear, others rush in blindly), the weightiness
of the impending decision, the state of your finances
at the moment, and so on.

Most of us are direct when there is nothing to
be anxious about, and each of us is circumspect—or
should be—on occasion. These are sensible, healthy
approaches to certainty or, as the case may be, to
reasonable doubt. A bit of both is necessary for any
investor. Too much of either at the wrong time can
create a spastic checkbook, with unpleasant results.

The most demonstrable—although by no means the
costliest—case of plunging and procrastinating I have
come across involved two men from my home town,
as it happens. Big Harry and Little Joe, let's call
them, were partners and at one time friends, until
too much prosperity spoiled what common interest
had earlier fashioned. A dozen years ago they were
earning enough to get by on as car salesmen in the
local Ford agency. Then Volkswagens began to venture
west of the major eastern port cities, and the possibilities
were quickly apparent to Big Harry and Little Joe.
Big Harry's wife's family had some property on which
they borrowed enough to qualify for a Volkswagen
dealership. A corporation was formed with the stock
divided into three equal shares, one third for Big
Harry, one third for Little Joe, and one third for
the capital raised by Big Harry. So, in effect, the
split was ⅔–⅓, which was perfectly agreeable to

all concerned at first, while both principals were putting in the same long hours and drawing identical salary and expenses, and as long as the profits were being plowed back into the business.

When the "beetle" began to catch on in the Midwest, Big Harry and Little Joe were ready to expand. By mortgaging the dealership to the bank they raised enough capital to become Volks distributors for south-central Ohio. Their interest in the business remained ⅔–⅓.

In a few short years, what had seemed like an equitable arrangement when profits were counted in thousands or even tens of thousands of dollars became galling to Little Joe as the net began to run into six figures. Little Joe felt that he had been used, if not actually duped, and that Big Harry was getting away with murder. Little Joe's wife came up with the idea that if Big Harry were a true friend and partner he would do "the right thing" now and let Little Joe put up the "few measly thousand bucks" to match Big Harry's initial capital outlay, so that the shares of the corporation could be redistributed on an "even-steven" basis.

But Big Harry and his wife didn't buy that idea. They felt that Little Joe was "damn lucky to get a free ride" on their money. In their opinion Little Joe would still be a "$150-a-week salesman in the Ford place" if it hadn't been for Big Harry and Big Harry's wife's father's property to back up their faith in the beetle to begin with.

Soon Big Harry and Little Joe found it advisable to restrict their relationship to business and even there to an irreducible minimum. Steadily, as Big Harry grew wealthy and Little Joe very comfortable, the latter's resentment increased. When, in January, 1968, they received a fair offer for their distributorship, there was no hesitation on the part of either man. After taxes, Big Harry netted $6 million, Little Joe half that amount.

Loaded with sudden cash and anxiety, both men sought investment opportunities. Big Harry went around saying that it pained him to think of all his millions working for the bank at higher rates of interest than the bank was paying him for the use of the money. Little Joe was talking mostly about the cost of putting six children through college and probably into business later on, besides taking care of his parents and his wife's mother for the rest of their lives.

The ex-partners still retained the same accountant as their tax and financial adviser, and after frequent but separate consultations, both accepted the same counsel: to invest about 40 percent of their funds in top-grade securities and about 40 percent in real estate, and to keep the remainder in the bank in the form of certificates of deposit and savings.

At the request of the accountant, a stockbroker had recommended a portfolio of seasoned "growth" stocks, quite suitable for Big Harry, who was seeking mainly to beat the bank rate of interest, but a shade conservative, perhaps, for Little Joe, who felt he needed to build up his capital to provide for numerous dependents. The selections were:

> American Tel & Tel
> Commonwealth Edison
> Pacific Gas & Electric
> Texaco
> Western Bancorporation

The investment plan proposed by the accountant and the broker jointly was for Big Harry to start by purchasing $200,000 worth of securities and then to continue putting in the same amount of money every month for a year. The plan for Little Joe was identical but at half the rate, or $100,000 a month.

Designed to reduce the risk of a sharp market decline in the near future, the plan gave Big Harry and Little Joe a chance to average out the cost of their purchases over twelve months, and thus to take advantage of lower prices later should there be a drop at any time during their investment period. Should their stocks go up during the year, of course, they would have to be prepared to pay higher prices and buy fewer shares. It is fundamental to the principle of dollar-cost-averaging that the investor incurs a loss if he discontinues his plan when the market value of his accumulated shares is less than his cost; and, concomitantly, that the investor benefits only if the average purchase cost of the shares is lower than the final sale price. Of course, no plan can protect against loss of value in severely depressed markets.

All things considered—in the spring of 1968 with stock prices rising and the economic barometer falling— the broker and the accountant agreed that it was wiser to play safe by dollar-cost-averaging than to commit all of the available funds immediately.

Although they had not seen each other since the sale of their business, Big Harry and Little Joe had been behaving in very similar manner: dazed, solemn and preoccupied. Now, however, when action was called for, a dissimilarity showed up.

Big Harry, who one might think would be rarin'

to take that first $200,000 out of the bank and put
it into securities which, with dividends and potential
price appreciation figured together, might earn him
double the bank interest alone, hesitated. While his
wife resorted to tranquilizers to quiet her queasy stom-
ach, Big Harry talked to another accountant and another broker, getting other ideas.

Little Joe, meanwhile, following the plan, put
$100,000 into the securities and amounts recommended.
It was not that Little Joe accepted responsibility calmly
—not by any means—just that he was glad to relieve
his unease by doing something positive. As he put
it, "Suddenly in a flash I saw myself as that stingy,
constipated character we're always making jokes about
—you know, the fellow that's still got the first quarter
he ever made because he hates to part with any
of it." Little Joe put off buying his wife the dream
house she'd already picked out, because he "wasn't
sure of the economy and money's gettin' so tight,"
but he had his check ready for the broker on the
morning of April 1.

On May 1 it was the same story. Big Harry was
still consulting other brokers, soliciting other ideas.
Little Joe wrote out a check and doubled his investment.

You may recall that during most of 1968 the direction
of stock prices was generally upward—the tail end
of the bull market, according to some economic fore-
casters. Little Joe, while pleased that the overall value
of his portfolio had increased, was also a little disturbed
that he was paying more for the very same stocks
that he could have bought earlier for less. He was
beginning to wonder whether his accountant and his
broker hadn't been too cautious and whether his in-

terests might not have been better served had he
gone for the whole $1,200,000 investment on April 1.

Nevertheless, on the first business day of each succeeding month Little Joe was ready and waiting with
his purchase money. But Big Harry was still "studying
the market," looking for "a definite trend," devouring
old as well as new recommendations from every broker
in town, comparing "track records" to help make up
his mind. Big Harry was in a sweat because he had
missed a good part of the market rise; at the same
time, reading about the clouding economic outlook
and the actions of the Federal Reserve in tightening
credit, he was also congratulating himself on having
avoided a "bath" by staying out of the market.

As of January 2, 1969, Little Joe had made ten
monthly investments totaling $1,008,153, including
brokerage commissions, and his portfolio stood like this:

Security	Cost to date	No. of shares	Per- centage gain	Per- centage yield
A.T.&T.	$ 201,626.56	3,839	+ 3.10	4.61
Com. Ed.	201,672.44	4,278	+ 3.40	4.71
Pacific G.&E.	202,034.75	5,826	+11.58	9.37
Texaco	200,936.19	2,480	+ 4.21	3.48
Western Banc	201,883.75	5,232	+ 9.28	3.14
TOTALS	$1,008,153.69	21,655	+ 6.31	4.06 av.

So, Little Joe's holdings were now worth about $63,000
more than he had put in and at the same time were
earning dividends at the indicated annual rate of over
4 percent, or $40,586.

Big Harry, painfully aware that procrastination had
cost him a sizable gain, was cussing out the gloomy

economists for having misled him. Any lingering doubts about committing his funds were now in exquisite balance with a gnawing conviction that the longer he waited the more dearly he would have to pay. Unable to see into the blurry future, certain only that right now others were profiting while he was not, on New Year's Eve Big Harry made a resolution in the presence of his wife and her family, and on January 2 he took the plunge. But instead of going in gradually, as planned, with $200,000 a month, he went the whole hog in order to make up for lost time. With an acute sensation of physical relief coupled with vague doomsday apprehension, he ordered his broker to purchase $2 million worth of the very same securities originally recommended to him.

Six weeks later, for no single ascribable cause, investor confidence suffered one of its recurrent sudden attacks of acute fades. Stock prices went skidding and tumbling in the worst market break in several years, with the Dow-Jones Industrial Average dipping about 5 percent in two weeks. Afterward this decline would be recognized as the first loud signal that the long bull market, which had been on its deathbed since 1965, was officially dead and that a long bear market was being born. At the time, however, nobody could be sure.

Little Joe was stricken with a terrible vision of his million-dollar-plus portfolio being carried away in an economic avalanche. Hitting the panic button, he sold every share he owned on February 20. Near collapse over what he regarded as a very close call, Little Joe came out with $1,118,633, a net profit of $9,648, not counting his income from dividends.

Big Harry, in contrast, was shocked into a state

of cataplexy by the sudden reversal. With the national economy smoking and the stock market sputtering, he, like many other investors, was unable to decide what to do or to do it. Here is how his portfolio looked at the end of February:

Security	Cost	No. of shares	Percentage loss
A.T.&T.	$ 403,308	7,476	−3.04
Com. Ed.	403,524	8,310	−1.04
Pacific G.&E.	403,988	10,560	−6.60
Texaco	402,280	4,790	−1.80
Western Banc	403,786	9,666	−5.74
TOTALS	$2,016,888.38	40,802	−3.64 av.

On paper, Big Harry was a quick loser by $73,013, or 3.64 percent. And it eased his calcified will not a whit to hear his broker point out (in his own defense) that even coming in late, in January 1969, had Big Harry limited his investment to $200,000 a month his losses in the February break would have been 90 percent less and he would still have $2.2 million with which to dollar-cost-average, come what may, through the balance of the year.

As Big Harry looked at it, he was an innocent victim of unpredictable circumstances. Had the market spurted up instead of down, he told his wife and her family, he would now be a big winner and a recognized financial genius. As it was, unfortunately, the options being pressed upon him were these: (1) to "realize" his losses by liquidating his holding; (2) to beef up his portfolio by replacing three stocks that were off the most; or (3) to sit tight until the market turned around, as it always had, eventually, in the past.

Gifted with twenty-twenty hindsight, we can plainly see that Big Harry might have done well to follow the lead of his erstwhile junior partner, Little Joe. But even after he recovered from his initial shock, Big Harry was still immobilized by concern over what his wife and her family might say if he were to be "bluffed out," as he put it, so soon after making the scene. And as a matter of record, Big Harry's paper losses were recouped in full when the market turned around again temporarily in the second quarter —thus providing him with a rationalization for standing pat, a posture that he managed to maintain through the next twelve trying months.

In April 1970, as an economic credibility gap opened up between businessmen and the administration in Washington, interest rates started to shoot up higher and stock prices nosedived another 60 points, leaving the Dow-Jones Industrial Average teetering precariously about 250 points below its crest of 985 in December 1968. All of a sudden the dam burst for Big Harry and his pent-up anxiety began to run. Just as he had plunged into the market after brooding over it for ten months, he now plunged out after brooding over it for sixteen months. His loss totaled $322,704, or 16 percent of his invested capital. Which said something for the relative quality of his holdings, at least, since the average was off by 25 percent during this time.

Two men, commencing an investment program with the same stocks and the same strategy at the same point in market history, end up with widely dissimilar financial results. It happens all the time, practically every time. Little Joe, who had exercised enough self-discipline to stick with a sound twelve-month plan for eleven months, quit in a panic but with a profit. He was lucky, maybe, but not *dumb* lucky, because while there is rarely any reason to buy stocks in a hurry, there may be very good reasons for selling without delay. Big Harry, on the other hand, paid a heavy penalty, because under the stress of making investment decisions he tended first to cramp up and then to let go all the way. From which we may conclude that, although plunging and procrastinating are two sides of the same coin, neither is apt to be heads up in the stock market.

4

Inside
the Insiders

This one is partly on me. A personal come-to-realize or investor's mirror of my own.

Without really thinking about it, I had always assumed that the insider was on the fast track. He had everything going for him. Along with intimate, often confidential, knowledge of a company, he had the advantage of surprise in timing his move either to buy or to sell. Besides, if insider information wasn't so desirable, why would its use and dissemination be restricted by rules and regulations? And why would intelligent men and women in positions of responsibility risk the penalties of violation at times by seeking to capitalize on insider information? Sensational headlines on the financial pages every now and then tended to reinforce my general impression that insider information belonged in the category of good things that were, unhappily, illegal, immoral or fattening.

Before I became associated with the investment business, I did a bit of wishful thinking, like some of my friends today who dream of the short cut. If I could get it straight from the horse's mouth—or from someone who did—I would have a chance to take a position at the outset of a promising situation instead of being obliged to watch and study and wait for a significant move to become apparent to me and, incidentally, to everyone else in the market. Like so many investors these days, I had the attitude that information written up, printed, and distributed by dozens, maybe hundreds, of brokers to thousands of their clients was already stale by the time it reached me. When the public was in on it, the profit was out of it. The lucky insider, however, could strike it rich, because he would be buying when the public was still selling, and then selling when everybody else was rushing in to buy.

This attitude stayed with me until I became an insider of a sort myself a number of years ago, when I had occasion to make a special study for one of the giants of American industry, the undisputed leader in its particular field, a company whose stock I had been accumulating in my own portfolio. My work, which took about two months to complete, brought me into daily contact with top management. I was impressed—if that's the word—with the mediocrity of the young new president as well as with the "team" selected by him. And by the time my study was written up and presented to the directors of the corporation, my first impression had hardened into conviction. Based on subjective size-up of people rather

than on objective consideration of financial data, with
which my study was not concerned, I was persuaded
that the company was definitely on the downgrade.
I sold my stock. Not only that, but over-reacting
because I was so disappointed in management, I put
the proceeds into the stock of a competitor, the No.
2 company in the industry.

What happened? Within six months the young new
president was replaced by a seasoned man with an
excellent record, and the executive committee was
reconstituted. The price of the stock picked up on
the news, and so did sales and earnings before long.
I had been right in my evaluation of management
but dead wrong just the same. Unfortunately for me.

While not an insider in the legal sense of using
or passing along "material facts" that might affect
anyone else's market decision, I had enjoyed a close-up
view. And I was fooled by it. I had missed the forest
for the trees. I did not anticipate that the directors
would act so quickly to rebuild a sluggish management
team, or that the market might respond so promptly
to an effective change-over. I knew something but
not nearly enough.

Just that, knowing something but not enough, has
proved to be the fatal weakness of many an insider.
While you may be privy to a great deal of pertinent
information about a company, its sales, its profits,
its plans for expansion, its new patents or explorations,
the company is only one part of a complex equation.
Another part is the industry and its prospects relative
to those of your company. And still another critical
part of the equation is the stock market, an entirely
different ball park. Knowledge of an increase in earnings
that might spark an insider may be irrelevant in a

market that is uninterested in the company or its industry, or is perhaps preoccupied in other areas. By the same token, the effect of poor earnings may be more than offset by market projection of the industry future or the general economic outlook.

Whatever privileged information an insider may possess, he is usually at the mercy of the unknowns and unanticipatables. The just-completed merger understanding may be challenged by the Justice Department. The revolutionary new process, still unannounced, may not work outside of the laboratory or, even if it does, may be made obsolete by a superior development by a competitor; or it may be a fine, workable exclusive and still remain unappreciated in the market until its efficiency is reflected in a reported earnings increase.

Just as a peek into the corporate kitchen may befuddle and mislead, oddly enough there are times when ethical considerations, as well as the regulations against using insider information, may be a very lucky break.

This is another one on me.

Not too long ago an old schoolmate came calling unexpectedly. Brad was—and still is—president and principal shareholder of a listed California company that he has built up from scratch. But he was not at all happy about it just then. While the industry was enjoying glamor status and price-earnings multiples of 30 times and more, Brad's company was priced at only 15 times earnings. To the owner of 650,000 shares priced at $18 a share, the differential was substantial; it was particularly galling to an aggressive, acquisitive businessman who was eager to grow by exchanging high-value paper for compatible plants and technical know-how that could add immediately to income and profits.

What Brad wanted of me, he announced at once, was just friendly, informal, no-obligation chitchat. Over dinner he disclosed that he was at a crossroads. He had three ways to go. He could continue building the slow, hard way, through steadily increasing sales and earnings; but this was not what he would choose to do if he could help it. Or he could acquire for shares one or two fledgling companies in his field, although, he pointed out, he would be getting no bargains at the present market valuation of his stock. Or he could go the opposite route and be acquired by a larger company. He had already received an offer to sell out at 20 times earnings, he confided. The deal had a drawback, however, in that it would retire him prematurely (he was then about forty) or reduce him to the status of an employee. No matter how much money he would take out of it—and Brad liked money—he had no intention of calling it quits just yet or working for anyone else. He was a builder and his own man, he insisted, and that was the way it was going to be as long as he had anything to say about it.

Since it was apparent that none of Brad's three options appealed to him strongly, I asked him if he had considered the possibility of selling some more of his stock in the company, not so much as to jeopardize his absolute control but enough to transform paper value into actual money and thus satisfy at least his desire to live like a rich man.

Brad replied firmly in the negative. He was not selling any of his stock—not a share—at 15 times earnings, he insisted. As if a sore point had been

touched, he began to run down investment bankers
in general and his own, a reputable firm that had
underwritten his initial stock offering, in particular.
All investment bankers were just interested in the
quick buck, he charged. His own had failed to support
his stock in the after-market, he felt, and so were
responsible for the present unrealistic price of the
shares. They had let him down, he stated flatly. Had
they done their job and continued to recommend his
stock to their clients after they had "collected their
underwriting profits," the stock would now be "way
up there," he asserted.

A supersalesman, Brad was overselling himself, I
suspected, distorting the facts to conform to his argument. I reminded him that his stock had come out
at $22 a share and had climbed as high as $43 before
sliding back. Since I had bought 200 shares myself
at $24 I was fairly familiar with the ups and downs
of the price. In all candor I told him that I didn't
see how his underwriters could be blamed for the
public's lack of enthusiasm for the company's subsequent rate of growth.

It was a no-decision meeting. After Brad returned
to California his stock remained on the skids, sliding
down as low as 9 where it bobbed about for several
months. From time to time I heard or read about
Brad negotiating mergers or acquisitions, none of which
ever panned out. Then the company earnings began
to show improvement and the price of the stock began
to climb. When and if it reached $24, my purchase
price, I would sell, I told myself. In common with
too many investors who develop a peeve against a
losing stock, all I wanted to do was to get even
and get out.

More than a year after our dinner conversation Brad phoned to say that he was contemplating switching investment bankers. Would my firm be interested in advising his company on financial matters? I put him in touch with one of my partners and again, as the months went by, forgot about Brad, although not about my investment in his company.

When the stock reached $24, my magic number, I was still set to sell, but since the price had been creeping up steadily by ¼ or ½ almost every day, I decided to watch closely for a while longer. At $27 the stock seemed to run out of support. This was my cue to take a profit. But before I could get around to placing the order I learned that my firm was going into registration with an offering to sell 200,000 shares, as managing underwriter. There was a question now whether I could legally and ethically sell my stock, having advance knowledge of Brad's public offering.

Legal counsel, which I sought, added up to this: selling my stock in advance of the underwriting would not violate any rules or regulations designed to protect the public; however, it could be construed as competing with Brad, an investment banking client—conflict of interest, in other words. I was advised to write Brad, explain the circumstances, and ask him to state for the record whether he would regard the sale of my 200 shares at this time as jeopardizing the success of his 200,000 share offering sometime during the next few weeks. It seemed ridiculous on the face of it: 200 shares "in competition with" 200,000! I did not write the letter. I could imagine Brad getting all steamed up about my picayune sale as further evidence of the opportunism of the investment banking frater-

nity. I resigned myself to keeping my stock until after
Brad's underwriting was fully distributed and taking
my chances in the after-market.

Meanwhile, the stock had resumed its upward crawl.
By the time Brad's 200,000 shares were offered to
the public, the price had reached $34. Keeping my
fingers crossed, I waited. Instead of dropping off after
the underwriting, as I had feared, the price continued
to rise. I finally sold my 200 shares at 45⅛, the historical
high.

Had I not been inhibited by insider considerations,
I would have been poorer by about $3,600!

Who is an insider? And just what is insider information? I don't know, though I've tried to find out.
The law doesn't really say, and the Securities and
Exchange Commission, if it knows, won't say unequivocally. So the issue is usually left up to the courts,
where we may as well leave it, also.

What is more meaningful for our purposes is whether
insider information is all that valuable or reliable—in
other words, whether the individual who seeks or
uses such information does better than one who does
not.

The securities laws, as we all know, advance the
principle of "full disclosure." The S.E.C., by its inter-
pretation and enforcement of the laws, has insisted
not only on full disclosure but also on prompt dissemination of "material facts." The aim is fair play. Give
every investor the same information at the same time.
It's like the start of a race. Everybody is in the same
starting position until the sound of the gun. No breaks,
no advantage to anyone on the track.

The intent of the law or of its enforcement agency is not in question here. But with heavy emphasis on full and prompt disclosure there is an underlying implication that to be in possession of the available facts is to be able to act wisely. This does not always square with experience.

Here is a case record, in brief, that goes to the heart of the matter. The president of an unlisted company of medium-small size (about $10 million in annual sales) has been trying for years to favor his family, whose financial support helped him start the business, by leaking tidbits of information about new contracts, earnings projections, and the like. His family has lost so much money by acting on these tips that only the most loving and naïve among them pay attention any longer. His own father, a retired gentleman in poor health, has dribbled away a small fortune by acting on "material facts" that were either immaterial as far as the market was concerned at the time or which had been thoroughly discounted. The company president may have a lot to say, but if the market isn't listening, he'd better not put his money on it.

The Killing of Quentin Quinton

Lest you think that I have been dealing from a stacked deck in an attempt to prove what sensational news stories seem to contradict, that there is never, never any advantage to be gotten from inside information, let me tell you about Quentin Quinton.

Before he was abruptly kicked out, Q.Q. held the position of senior vice president and management supervisor in a well-established "top-ten" advertising

agency. One of the important accounts that Q.Q. su-
pervised was a national magazine which from time
to time had been acting frantic in the race for cir-
culation and advertising revenue. After helping to
stamp out cancer by stomping on the tobacco companies
for several issues, the magazine took sick from the
drug industry for a while, and then did its part to
make highways safe for foreign cars by running down
the auto industry in Detroit. Now it was about to
bite down hard on a common household item almost
as useful and profitable as soap, with annual sales
in the billions. The teeth of the exposé were the
findings of an independent testing laboratory, which
rated all popular brands of the item in the order
of their reported harmful effects. Only one brand,
XYZ, with a tiny fraction of the market, came through
as relatively safe.

All this was supposed to be hush-hush, of course,
until publication day, except that Quentin Quinton
regularly received advance proofs of feature editorial
matter, for the purpose of directing the preparation
of advertising designed to stimulate newsstand sales
of the magazine. And the moment Q.Q. glanced at
his proofs he recognized an opportunity of a lifetime.
It was instantly apparent to him that XYZ Company,
makers of the safe-rated brand, would get a tremendous
sales boost from the exposé and that, much more
significant to Q.Q., its stock, listed on the Big Board,
would soar as soon as the magazine hit the stands.

Dropping everything else, Q.Q. started seeking cash
with which to buy XYZ stock. As usual, however,
his capital was tied up in a number of long-shot
ventures, from thoroughbred horse breeding in Virginia
to sugar beet experiments in Maine. But XYZ seemed

like such a sure thing that Q.Q. was willing to sell
anything he owned and even go into hock, if necessary,
in order to take a big position in the stock before
the news broke. But as luck would have it, he was
locked in tight; there were no ready cash buyers for
what he had to sell.

Two days before the magazine issue date, Q.Q.
had managed to scrape up only enough money to
buy 200 shares of XYZ Company at $23 a share,
on margin. Desperate, he phoned his wife from the
office and confided in her. He begged her to mortgage
the house, which was in her name, pawn her jewels,
close out her personal savings account and borrow
all she could from her family, that very same day,
and lend it all to him. He promised on his word
of honor to cut her in on the "biggest thing that
had ever happened" to him. But Mrs. Quinton said
that she was awfully sorry, she just couldn't help
him. For the next forty-eight hours Q.Q. tore around
the city in a frenzy, trying to borrow large sums
without giving his angle away. But no dice.

On publication day, just as Q.Q. had anticipated,
the market reacted immediately and dramatically to
the magazine exposé. While the stocks of all the lower-
rated brands plummeted, XYZ took off like a rocket.
By the close it had doubled and the next day it
went over 100. The third day XYZ reached 144, and
Q.Q. was too sick at heart to do any work. He went
home right after the close of the market to seek his
wife's commiseration over the once-in-a-lifetime opportunity they had missed. He had been in the right
place at the right time, he had read the odds right—yet
all he had to show for it was a gain of about $24,000.

Peanuts—considering the killing he might have made had he been able to put his hands on any real money.

Mrs. Q., however, seemed quite sanguine about the whole thing. This was the last straw for Q.Q. Losing his temper, he told his wife what he thought of her and of her indifference to his disappointment.

When at last he was done, she replied calmly in words to this effect: "I want to thank you, Quentin, for suggesting that I mortgage the house and pawn my jewels and close out my savings account and borrow money from my family. I did just what you said. And I invested every penny of it in XYZ stock, just as you said, too. Now, you worthless, cold-blooded two-timer, I have enough money to get along without you. So, you can pack your bags right this minute and leave my house. Your lawyer will be hearing from my lawyer in the morning. Oh yes, and while you're at it, you might as well look for a new job, because I intend to blow the whistle on you at the agency and let them know just what kind of dishonest, untrustworthy skunk you are."

At last report, Q.Q. was peddling radio time for a small New England network in which he had an interest.

As suggested earlier, it's not that insiders *never* profit from the use of privileged information, rather that the outcome is far from certain; and there is always the side hazard of risking more than money.

In fact, an insider is often at a disadvantage in relation to outsiders. Just to give you an idea, here are some of the ethical hurdles confronting your own stockbroker.

No matter what he knows about a situation, your broker may not compete with his clients. And he may not use your buy or sell order to influence the market in his own favor, even inadvertently. On the contrary, he must put your interests ahead of his own. When a "hot" new issue comes to market, your broker is really on the outside looking in, because he may not buy any new issue for himself or his immediate family until the demands of all other clients have been satisfied. And when bright new ideas originate in his own research department, your broker may not buy one share of the recommended stock for himself or his family until the public has been given reasonable time to receive, digest and act upon the information.

Still willing to take your chances on a tip from an insider?

Over four decades ago—before the present laws blunted the edge of any insider advantage—William P. Hamilton, editor of *The Wall Street Journal,* who refined the well-known Dow Theory, made some still-pertinent observations:

> These so-called "insiders," the real men who conduct the real business of a corporation, are too busy to spend their time over the stock ticker. They are far too limited, too restricted to their particular trade, to be good judges of the turn of the market. They are normally bullish on their own property, in the respect that they believe it to be a growing concern with great possibilities. But of

the fluctuations of business which will affect their stock, together with the rest of the same group or all other railroad and industrial stocks in the same market, their view is singularly limited. It is not mere cynicism but truth to say that sufficient inside information can ruin anybody in Wall Street.

Bernard Baruch, who had reason to feel even more strongly about it, writes in his autobiography, *My Own Story:* "The longer I operated in Wall Street the more distrustful I became of tips and 'inside' information of every kind. Given time, I believe that inside information can break the Bank of England or the United States Treasury."

5

Little Old Young Ladies in Tennis Shoes/ Fearful Young Men in Their Flying Machines

Fear is a prime mover and shaper of investing instincts.

There is fear of losing money. A familiar feeling. We hate to lose a dollar even if we have enough not to notice the loss. Chauncey Depew—one of our richer millionaires—once declared that while he would not give any thought to earning another thousand dollars, he would stay up late every night for a week to keep from losing a hundred.

There is also fear of making a mistake and being dismissed as a wastrel or laughed at as a fool. This kind of fear is particularly marked among new investors whose friends are more experienced and, perhaps, already successful in the market. Beginners often fear loss of dignity or prestige along with their money.

Among some there is fear of a psychological hang-up.

Losers in business or marriage or football pools may be afraid to close the circle on themselves, in effect, by proving to be losers in yet one more significant (to them) area. They go into a stock with a negative attitude, hoping not to lose too much *this* time. For the half-beaten and the pessimist, the market can be something extra fearful.

Sometimes there are deeply rooted fears, manifestations of insecurity, as they say, and for those so possessed, loss of money (purchasing power) is supposed to be code for loss of procreative powers, or painfully reminiscent of the loss of a parent in childhood.

None of which is meant to knock good old-fashioned prudence. Fear is one thing; prudence and conservatism, the traditional small arts of self-preservation, are something else again. A large percentage of investors, for purely financial considerations, have no sensible choice but to be conservative. Yes, widows and orphans; and retired people for whom regular dividends are a source of needed income; even young people building for the future but lacking sufficient cash reserves to provide a margin for error have no business being frisky about their investments. Prudence is always appropriate. Fear can be a serious handicap.

The excessively timid soul is a curious commonplace to brokers—so much so that one prominent brokerage firm has undertaken a motivational study of "infrequent" and "small" investors. Interviews in depth indicated two strains or styles of personality pattern: the passive and the proud. The passive individual seems to be fearful of being led or pushed over some psychological precipice. The proud appears to have reservations, even guilt feelings, about money making money (as opposed to brains or talent or muscle making money).

Each of the timid souls interviewed in the study shared one or more of these investment traits:

1. He prefers to do business with an older, more experienced broker working for a larger, better known brokerage firm, and to hold shares of older, well established, long-time dividends-paying companies in "respectable" or basic industries.

2. He finds it difficult to decide what stocks to buy, sell or hold, how much or when.

3. Even though he is dependent on others for ideas and advice, the timid soul is suspicious when his broker phones, and wary about any suggestions offered.

4. He has a long-range goal—five years or longer—but doesn't really expect to reach it. And if he does reach his goal, he is inclined to regard his achievement as undeserved or lucky or even as something to be ashamed of.

5. He takes the attitude that saving in a bank is virtuous and that investing in securities is gambling.

6. Though he worries about his investments, he sits with them, out of "loyalty" to his commitments or fear of making any change.

In each of the three investment case reports that follow you may decide for yourself whether the protagonist is prudent or fearful, passive or proud, his own best friend or worst enemy. If you admit to reservations or fears of your own, you may be able to recognize a companion symptom or two and—who knows?—even a common cause.

Little Old Young Ladies in Tennis Shoes

In the same advertising agency where earlier we met Quentin Quinton the insider, there are two very solid citizens whose investment habits are quite different. We'll start with the lady. Alice, who is the creative head of a group of accounts—mostly in the women's field—is very good at her job, well liked, and about as secure as it is possible to be in the advertising business, having worked for the same agency for fifteen years. She is compensated, I would guess, at $1,000 a week plus participation in a 15 percent profit-sharing retirement plan and other fringe benefits.

Early in her career Alice had observed that new clients nearly always racked up sales increases during the first year or two of their association with the agency. Whether because of superior advertising, as Alice chose to believe, or more aggressive marketing or for other reasons, share of market usually improved dramatically, for a while at least. Acting on her observations, Alice had developed a pattern of buying the stocks of the agency's new clients. She was motivated by pride in the agency, loyalty and a desire to show her support for the team, especially when the new client was one assigned to her group; but at the same time Alice was shrewdly aware of the financial opportunities presented by growth companies. This latter point should be stressed, because I know how thoroughly Alice investigated before she invested, invariably obtaining research opinions from her broker and afterwards asking questions that showed how care-

fully she had read the words and studied the numbers—
no matter how strongly her heart was preset on making
the investment anyway. Often Alice continued her
investigations right up to the date the first new ad
campaign was scheduled to break. And then what?
For each and every company Alice gave her broker
an order to buy exactly $1,000 worth of stock, no
more, no less, or about 20 shares on the average.

How do you explain it? An unmarried lady under
forty, with no dependents or financial obligations,
highly skilled and highly paid, with as much as $150,000
vested in a profit-sharing retirement plan, interested
in capital gains, imbued with a sense of loyalty for
the agency's clients, especially her own accounts, forti-
fied usually by a favorable opinion from her broker,
who could never bring herself to risk a penny more
than $1,000! Or look at it another way. In her invest-
ment experience Alice had had few losers, none serious,
and a number of winners including several substantial
ones. On the record, shouldn't she show more confidence
in her own intuition and knowledge?

Actually Alice has a pretty good system—as systems
go—because she has seen creative advertising influence
consumer demand and ultimately company profits; and
she is competent to judge the sales clout of a new
advertising campaign before it hits the consumer. Yet
she tiptoes through her opportunities in tennis shoes
when another in her position might come on like
gangbusters.

Little Old Young Men in Tennis Shoes

Dr. John, Ph.D., the agency's director of research, is relatively new at his job. A bachelor in his early thirties and already an economist of note, he earns just about as much as Alice, I would guess. Dr. John has access to much the same information as Alice; he also has the advantage of economic and industrial perspective to guide him in selecting a particular company for investment. But Dr. John does not buy the securities of any of the agency's clients, not their stocks or their bonds. In fact, he buys not one share of stock in any publicly owned corporation. (The agency by which he is employed is privately owned.) The only securities that Dr. John considers for investment purposes are municipal bonds. And his reasons are presented forthrightly, almost vehemently. Dr. John takes a dim view of the way the economy is trending. He fears creeping socialism, the encroachment of government on business, the stranglehold of organized labor on industry and government, and the dissipation of the purchasing power of savings, pensions, insurance and fixed incomes as a consequence of unchecked inflation. But more than anything else, he fears and hates the pernicious institution of a steeply graduated income tax. As he puts it, "I have no faith in any securities, the way things are going, but you've got to say this for municipal and state bonds—if they default, money won't be worth much anymore anyway. And at least until they go down, the interest is exempt from federal and New York state income tax. That's my biggest satisfaction, getting back at them through their own debt obligations."

Emotional satisfaction apart, how does Dr. John fare financially? Filing a return as a single man on a salary of $50,000, he is probably in the 60 percent income tax bracket. Based on 1970 tax rates, a 5.50 percent municipal bond nets him the equivalent of 13.75 percent income from a taxable source, such as stock dividends or bank interest—that is, if he could find a bank to pay him over 13 percent on his deposits or a good common stock offering that kind of yield.

No question about it, Dr. John is smart to be in municipal bonds. But all the way? Isn't he overdoing a good thing? While he is beating the government out of a few thousand dollars a year, tops, he is also beating himself out of a future estate. If he were not so fearful of an imminent collapse of all the economic forces, he would probably be investing part of his surplus funds in growth equities. He can well afford the risks and is much too savvy not to realize that during the past five years while he was titillating himself with tidy tax exemptions, he was also missing a great chance to double his capital in common stocks. As they used to say before devaluation fuzzed the difference, "penny wise, pound foolish."

"Courage and cowardice are the same instinct, only one smells better than the other," I was once told by a physician who had served as a medical officer in the German army. Cowardice may be much too strong a word to describe what ails investors like Alice and Dr. John, who bypass opportunity after opportunity without grabbing a handful, but certainly the virus is a variety of fear. Dr. John may be scaring himself silly with his own economic forecasts. But

Alice is convinced, with reason, that she should invest in the new clients of a fine advertising agency that has helped make winners of other companies in the past. She believes strongly that creative advertising is as essential to sales as sales are to earnings. What Alice lacks to go with her conviction is the courage thereof.

Fearful Young Men in Their Flying Machines

Courage is one thing nobody could ever say was lacking in my friend Halsey. Let me give you some nonfinancial background. I first met Halsey in 1943 in a bombproof conference room in the basement of McNair Hall at Fort Sill, Oklahoma, where we were assigned to prepare a new War Department Manual, *FM 6-150, Field Artillery Organic Air Observation.* Halsey was then a light colonel, about twenty-seven or twenty-eight years old, just out of the hospital after being badly busted up in North Africa, and scornful of our "pen pushing" assignment. He had been picked for the job, he said, because he was the first army officer dumb enough to fly a Piper Cub off the deck of an aircraft carrier.

It had been Halsey's mission to establish a Corps Artillery Air OP in the Casablanca racetrack in the first hours of the North African campaign. According to Halsey's account, as soon as he took off from the flight deck of the *Ranger* in his L-3, a low-performance artillery spotter capable of a top speed of 125 miles an hour, the entire U.S. fleet opened fire on him. Having never seen a Cub a few hundred feet overhead, the Navy antiaircraft gunners evidently mistook the

L-3 for an enemy bomber at higher altitude. With the flak bursting above him, Halsey managed to get over the beach, where he immediately came under the fire of our landing forces. Escaping into the interior, he became the target of enemy antiaircraft. Finally, as he was slipping into the Casablanca racetrack where he was to rendezvous with his ground crew (which was supposed to be making its way overland) Halsey was hit and brought down. A broken back was the most serious of his injuries. "So I'm the army's expert on conducting artillery fire from the air," he told me sourly. "I never got to call a single shot in anger."

I'll say flatly that Halsey was the gutsiest human I've ever known. When he was five his parents were killed in an auto crash. An only child, he was left with a half million dollars in high-grade bonds and a grandmother who raised him lovingly. By the age of fourteen Halsey was "borrowing" automobiles that he would race against anyone on the highway. (If you're not old enough to remember that in the twenties there was no such thing as a driver's license or minimum age requirements in many states, please take my word for it.) Soon he was on motorcycles. While he liked girls—very much!—his passion was for speed. Before long he had graduated to airplanes. An uninhibited daredevil, he took to stunting, which led him eventually to aerial acrobatics at county fairs and to barnstorming jaunts around the Midwest during summer vacations. His grandmother, who let him have his way about almost everything else, insisted on his going to college. Gifted mechanically, he breezed through Purdue to take a degree in engineering, then went to work for Ford as a general supervisory handyman and test pilot on the old trimotor transport.

Meanwhile his grandmother, ignoring the advice of banker and lawyer, had sold about 20 percent of Halsey's inheritance, all in gilt-edge bonds, and invested the proceeds in common stocks—which was about as irresponsible, not to say radical, as a custodian could get with the estate of an orphan in those days. The stocks she bought, of course, were the bluest of the blue chips, each and every one represented among the 30 Dow-Jones Industrials. As a consequence, when the old lady died in 1939, Halsey's worth had increased from a half million dollars to three quarters of a million.

A reserve officer in the field artillery (R.O.T.C.), Halsey was called to active duty in 1940. He made every effort to obtain a transfer to what was then called the Army Air Corps, but failed and had to content himself, but barely, as a motor transport officer. At this juncture of his life he was apparently drinking a lot and wenching a lot (the only thing Halsey ever bragged about), until he met Nancy, the sweet, strong, devoted girl he promptly married. But even Nancy couldn't block out the death wish or whatever it was that drove him to risk his neck in any kind of vehicle, just as long as it went fast, alone or in competition. He raced his brother officers in jeeps, prime movers or private cars, on paved roads, on the proving grounds or on the post golf course at night in blackout. After the United States got into the war Halsey learned that the field artillery was experimenting with Air OPs, or aerial forward observers, and volunteered. He had a ball outgliding, outstunting and out-puddle-hopping his instructors at the Air Corps primary school.

On receiving his L- (for Liaison pilot) wings, Halsey

was designated division artillery liaison officer with
the school troops at Fort Sill. Flying an L-1, he
spotted targets for officers and gun crews in training.
The L-1, or T-craft, had a bad habit of spinning
in under 200 feet, which endeared it to Halsey, because
the hazards of landing gave him a special thrill. When
after several fatal accidents, the L-1 was replaced
by the much more stable L-2 (Aeronca) and L-3
(Piper Cub), Halsey became bored after a while.
He was absolutely delighted to be chosen the top
field artillery spotter in the North African campaign.
Characteristically, he ordered himself to be the first
L-pilot in the air.

Which brings us back to the underground conference
room at Fort Sill, where Halsey, just a few months
out of the hospital and permanently grounded because
of his back injury, was still resisting his reclassification
to limited service. Somehow or other he could always
wangle a plane at the post airfield and would go
waggling his wings at Nancy over their rented house
in Lawton. Or else he would hang around the auto
sales agencies and service stations in town in his big,
beautiful 1939 Buick Roadmaster hunting unwary Cad-
illacs to race on a two-mile stretch of road he had
reconnoitered from the air. As you can imagine, *FM
6-150* was a long, long time in preparation. I honestly
believe the only reason Halsey and I became friends
was because when my '39 Mercury started making
ugly sounds I took it to Halsey instead of to the
local dealer. After he'd made it purr like a pussy
cat, Halsey challenged me to a race, gallantly offering
me the choice of weapons, my Mercury or his Buick.

When we became close enough so that I could
get a glimpse of Halsey's financial side, the first thing

that struck me was his nervous attitude about money.
He never played cards or shot crap like most of us—
okay. But he never bet on anything, not even on
himself. His racing was strictly for sport or for self-
destruction, whichever way you care to interpret it;
he would not risk a nickel on the outcome. Although
Nancy could always have anything she wanted, if
it cost money she had to ask for it first and sometimes
more than once. He was such a thin tipper that even
his friends avoided going out to dinner with him.
It was not merely that Halsey was stingy. Despite all
the wealth socked away in his bank vault back home, he
acted as if he had nothing in the world but his Army
pay. And yet, curiously, Halsey had not looked at his
portfolio of stocks and bonds since his grandmother's
death. He couldn't even say what he owned.

Now, neglect of a portfolio for four years would
have to be regarded as imprudent at any period of
time but especially so when the entire economy had
been forced to make a sudden transition from total
peacetime production to almost total war production.
There was hardly a major industry or major company
whose fortunes had not been affected for better or
for worse, temporarily or for many years to come,
with the bombing of Pearl Harbor. Halsey's locked-
away securities represented financial risks and financial
opportunities of a substantial sort. Yet apart from the
fact that his portfolio had been worth about $750,000
in 1939 and now consisted of two thirds bonds and
one third stocks, Halsey could say little about his
holdings, not even whether he had made or lost money
in the four years since. The truth was, I believe,
that Halsey was scared silly to find out.

You may be more charitable and attribute Halsey's

attitude to the war: he was too busy with life and death
to be bothered with stocks and bonds. Or you might
be profoundly sentimental and say that the death and
wreckage of war had brought him back painfully close
to the death of his own parents. How could he think
about his money making money when in his memory-
wracked mind the world was on a collision course with
itself? And when it all came to a crashing halt, he clearly
intended to be right up front in the very nose of the
cataclysm. The only thing he was determined to leave
intact if not safe was his net worth.

At one time I had the idea that Halsey's hands-off
policy towards his inheritance signified distrust of the
stock market. Many people of his age and mine retained
a vivid recollection of the Great Crash. But apparently
his fears were not all that specific, as I discovered when
I asked him once why he didn't invest the cash dividends from his blue chips in more shares of the same
companies instead of sticking the money away in his
savings account. "Too risky," he replied, "enough in
stocks now." I asked him what good thing wasn't risky.
"Nothing" he conceded, shaking his head sadly, "even
the banks failed in '32." So he was leery even of leaving
his money in the bank.

In 1944 Halsey was separated from the Army and
went to work as an engineer in Detroit. Although his
back was so bad that his private pilot's license had been
lifted, he grabbed every chance to test-drive cars, especially the experimental models.

Industry was making the transition from war to
peace, and profound changes had taken place—new industries created, old industries obsolesced; atomic energy had made its debut, airlines and trucking were up,
railroads were down; computers and electronics and TV

were about to emerge as supergiant industries. Still
Halsey's prewar securities remained unchanged and
unlooked at. What was good enough for his grandmother was good enough for him. Until today, as far as
I can tell, Halsey's common stock portfolio remains as
it was at his grandmother's death, except for the ac-
cumulation of additional shares through stock dividends, a circumstance beyond his control. The bonds, of
course, have all matured by this time and been converted into cash, about a half million dollars, drawing
interest from forty or fifty savings banks.

So much for Halsey the man. Let's take a look at
Halsey the shareholder and see if we can get a fair
grasp of what he has done—or not done—with his
stocks, even though we don't know exactly which he
holds.

Since the death of Halsey's grandmother in 1939 the
purchasing power of the dollar has shrunk roughly 60
percent because of inflation. Halsey is paying about
$5,000 today for a car of the same relative quality that
cost him $2,000 then. While inflation has been a con-
tinuing trend, the cost of living has increased at variable
rates, some years faster, some years slower; over the
thirty years we are reviewing, at the rate of about 3
percent a year, and more recently at about 6 percent.
During this prolonged inflationary period the dollar has
lost buying power every year except two—1949 and
1955. Which suggests that before and after Halsey's
bonds redeemed themselves at 100 cents on the dollar
and found their way into his savings banks, the rate of
interest he received—mostly 3½ to 4 percent—barely
exceeded the rate of inflation. While Halsey was gaining
relative safety, he was losing a fabulous opportunity.

For during these same thirty years the economy was

growing at a fantastic rate which was fully reflected in the rise of common stock values. Just to give you an idea: In 1940 the Dow-Jones Index of 30 Industrial Stocks—traditionally, conservative high-grade issues—stood at about 131. In 1969 the same index closed at about 800—a rise of 510 percent. In other words, if Halsey's blue chips were appreciating at the same rate as the D.J.I. Average, by the end of 1969 his quarter-of-a-million-dollar common stock portfolio would have been worth over a million and a quarter! And if carefully tended as conditions and prospects changed, the resulting increase might have been even more dramatic.

But that's not all. At the same time that the value of his common stocks was probably being multiplied by a factor of five, he was also receiving dividends from his blue chips. Again, using the Dow-Jones Industrial Average as an indicator, in 1940 the dividends generated by the 30 D.J.I. stocks came to $7.06; by 1969, they had reached $33.90—a rise of 380 percent. Which suggests that Halsey's dividends—once more assuming that his stocks were paying out at the rate of the D.J.I. Average—had offset the 60 percent loss of purchasing power of the dollar by about six times!

To stretch the point a bit by way of illustration, let's say that Halsey had not neglected his inheritance, that he was actually being prudent and respectful of his grandmother's foresight in holding on to all his bonds until maturity. But what about after maturity? What about the proceeds? Instead of reposing in the banks, earning just about enough interest to stand off the inflationary squeeze, suppose the money had been reinvested, at least in part, in grandma's tried-and-true blue chips? Halsey might have cashed in on some of the lushest opportunities in our history.

So there we have the daringest man I have ever known. Absolutely fearless physically. Chicken financially. Bad back and all, he will still race anybody in anything on wheels but he still won't risk a dime (prewar nickel) on the outcome.

As a one-time pilot, Halsey realizes the importance of taking regular "fixes" on a course of action so as to calculate whether he is still headed where he wants to go, how far he still has to go to reach his destination, and how long it should take him to get there; but he has yet to do anything about his financial course.

Halsey's portfolio, in the language of our friendly neighborhood psychiatrist, is "guilty money" that he cannot touch, because it came to him as a consequence of the death of his parents. And closer to the surface, there is the dictum of the German army doctor: "Courage and cowardice are the same instinct," etc. Whatever the explanation for Halsey—and granted, he may be an extreme case—the fact remains that he is but one of many, many brave men who continue to back away from the risk of participating in the richest growth era ever seen in this or any other country.

6

Junk Dealers/
10-Percenters and
Bargain Hunters

What's the difference between a bargain and a junk stock?

Investment value.

Price alone gives you only one dimension in a multi-dimensional picture—the result of the interaction of supply and demand in the marketplace. Investment value, by contrast, is worth, or an appraisal of worth, usually based on another dimension, such as earnings, actual or potential. Since, over time, price and value tend to coincide, the value-conscious investor looks for stocks whose current worth appears to be substantially greater than the present price. The junk dealer, on the other hand, buys low price, as such, in the dismal and mistaken expectation that he "can't get hurt too much."

One company whose stock is selling at a price-earnings multiple well below that of the industry and the market as a whole may be a bargain at $500. While a $5 stock, measured by the same two-dimensional yardstick of price-earnings, may be dear at half the price.

A stock may be "cheap" for any number of good reasons that can spell the difference between junk and bargain. Here are some third dimensions culled from opinions by research analysts on a single day recently:

"Additional conglomerate merger attempts have muddied the waters."

"Earnings per share cut back by costs of starting up new machine and other improvements."

"Gold exploration halted by international bickering."

"Sulphur weakness is a negative short-term factor, ditto a drag on earnings."

"Decline due to cancellation of government contract plus tooling-up costs on new landing gear contract."

"Merger will result in small dilution."

"Cost pressures hold despite sales increase."

"Unsettled Peruvian political scene clouds outlook for earnings gain expected as a result of increased crude production."

"Poor profits due to weak demand for high-margined tantalum products and heavy R.&D. costs."

"Price off due to technical factors."

The given reason, if correct, may clear up the picture or it may blow sand in your eyes. You can't fight the tape, as they say. But also (as they say) there's nothing so changeable as sentiment in the stock market: a company or industry out of favor this afternoon may be tomorrow's darling deluxe—but don't count on it!

Pedigree can help you here, often. Another dimension. A company whose management has shown the ability to produce profits under competitive conditions in previous years must be given a better chance to "turn around" after a slump than an unseasoned company or one with a spotty record.

All of which may be obvious to you and to me. But *price* is still the bell ringer with a high percentage of investors.

A wealthy widow living in Florida feels bored and aimless. She trades stock 1,000 shares at a time because it gives her a feeling of accomplishment and something to do. In order to keep active in 1,000-share lots, however, she must limit herself to stocks priced at or under $10. Including low-priced new issues when she can get any, she takes a profit, on average, four times out of ten. On balance she is paying heavily for her involvement. To make up her losses and sustain her illusion of being at the center of things, she buys more and more cheapies. For a few dollars a throw, she has caught a ride on a costly merry-go-round.

10-Percenters

The very ambitious wife of a New York millionaire spends part of every weekday in a brokerage boardroom. Having grown up in the slums, she is keenly conscious of quality, although not yet completely at home with it. She always buys for value, on the advice of a bank officer. But not too sure of herself or her money, she relies on a fairly common system, settling for 10 percent either up or down—about five points on average. Although she has a very high percentage of winners, about seven out of ten, commissions in and out about 1 percent each way—eat into the differential between small gains and small losses. To explain why she has so little profit to show for so many winners and so much activity, she falls back on the old saw: "You can't go broke taking a profit." With her "safety" system and her investment adviser (to say nothing of her husband's reserves) she will never go broke, probably, but neither will she ever realize her ambitions. Her 10 percent system is just plain incompatible with her goal of high gains, which would entail taking the higher risks of holding on to her winners until their price comes close to her (or her adviser's) appraisal of their market worth.

Junk Dealers

A young and talented designer of high-fashion women's clothes shops stocks the way he used to select food or wine or cars before he was "discovered." He "makes do" with cheaper brands, hoping to trade up to quality someday when he can afford it and really knows what he is buying. He is being naïve, needless to say. In the stock market you never trade *up* to quality; you always trade *in* it—fine quality or poor quality but always quality. When he wises up—if he doesn't get discouraged first—he will realize that the cheapest stock is the one that gives him the most value for each dollar spent, regardless of price.

It may be going too far to say that the investor behaves as he does in the market (as in business) because of what occurred in his crib or on his toidy, but it is not totally irrelevant. In many cases the quickest clue to investor behavior is child psychology.

Gilbert was a desperately poor boy blessed with a near-genius IQ and two older brothers with even higher IQ's. Gilbert got the hand-me-downs and leftovers and almost no praise from his parents. During one period of his childhood he literally went without shoes. Although he was awarded a scholarship by an Ivy League school, he was too poor and too doubtful of himself to accept the opportunity. So Gilbert went to work right out of high school to help support his older brothers in college. His first job was in a used-garment, or thrift, shop in Philadelphia. Because he had a keen mind and from long experience could tell the value of castoffs almost instinctively, Gilbert did well. In a few years he had his own shop, and then a chain of shops selling marked-down "preworn" furs and dress clothes. But even as he prospered, Gilbert continued to buy for his own use factory-reject shoes and shirts, broken-lot suits, second-hand cars, and rebuilt appliances at discount—when he couldn't get them wholesale. It was no longer a matter of thrift, it was a behavior pattern deep-set in childhood.

When Gilbert ventured into the stock market he naturally looked for cheapies, "remnants" and "discards" at fire sale prices. He did make several shrewd buys, as it turned out eventually, but even when he was right about the issues he was wrong in terms of timing. His stocks went nowhere while he held them, because he was running counter to market sentiment. Even though a $5 Powder River Mining or a $2 Gold Plate Explorations might have intrinsic value, unless and until its worth is at least suspected by other investors the stock stagnates. And Gilbert lacked either the patience or the self-confidence to wait indefinitely for the market to catch up to him. So he took losses unnecessarily.

When Gilbert was forty years old and very wealthy (not from the market, however), he felt he was in a sufficiently secure position financially to take a chance on diminishing the drive that had helped him get where he was, and he decided to indulge himself in psycho-analysis—though on a cut-rate group basis. Two years later Gilbert was certified adjusted, "copable," and, believe it or not, really seemed to be a new man. Gone, for one thing, was the predilection for the used and the preworn at knocked-down prices. Almost the first thing Gilbert did after graduating from the group was to go to a custom tailor and order a complete new wardrobe, including his first leisure clothes. Next he bought a new Cadillac, his first new car. Then he told his stockbroker that he wanted to build a "respectable portfolio" of blue chips exclusively, price no object.

On the evidence, Gilbert had never lacked the ability to differentiate between value and cost, only the financial and emotional security to act upon his own judgment.

Bargain Hunters

Dear is not always superior to cheap, of course; and blue chips are not necessarily the best buys. As an investor, Harold bore some resemblance to the early Gilbert, but only superficially. Growing up in a family scrap business that eventually became a well-financed used-machinery concern, Harold was trained to inspect bankrupt factories and to appraise their equipment for liquidation purposes. He learned how to buy used ma-

chinery at the bottom dollar, how to have it rebuilt
"good as new," and how to sell it at the top dollar.
When he became interested in the stock market, Harold took a characteristic approach. He hunted down
shaky situations, studying the financial data and ap-
praising the assets, including plant and inventory, as if
the company were about to be liquidated. And when he
found a bargain, that is, an undervalued stock, he
bought all he could get at his price. If investor sentiment was not yet ready to recognize his estimate of
worth, Harold held the stock in inventory, that is, in
his portfolio, and waited for the market to come to him.
Always buying "liquidation value," the cheaper the
better, Harold did as well in the market, in terms of
return on invested capital, as in his own business.

Copeland's attitude and approach are almost dia-
metrically opposed to Harold's, yet equally effective.
Cope believes that just because a stock is cheap—in
terms of price range—is very good grounds to assume
that it will not soon be anything else. As he reasons, a
down-trending stock has a better than 50–50 chance to
continue going down. By the same token, he reasons,
an up-trending stock has better than a 50–50 chance
to continue going up. Cope likes to have his judgment
confirmed in advance.

A prominent newspaper man, Cope noses around for
small to medium-size companies with strong, upbeat
characteristics: bright, highly motivated management
with substantial personal holdings or options for company stock; a consistent record of increased earnings;
and a price-earnings multiple well below the industry

and market average. These criteria, Cope felt several years ago, were met by Holiday Inns, and a long jump ahead of the market he took a position in the stock. About the time the investment clubs were discovering Holiday Inns, Cope was putting his profits into Dow Jones.

Cope shuns the blue chips as well as the cats and dogs, by the way, arguing that since the institutions have replaced the traders as prime movers and shakers in the market, the public investor has little influence on big price movements of widely held stocks. Barring an ideal situation, as he sees it, where a blue chip is closely held, say 20 percent, by family and management, and other big chunks are on the books of institutions, Cope prefers to put his money where an order for a few hundred shares can still move the price.

Class will tell, he is convinced, and a company that is already on the high road is a better investment than another one that must turn around first to get there, regardless of size. Consistent in his method and confident of his own judgment, Cope does very well by concentrating on *emerging* quality.

Numerous strategies of brilliant variety for buying stocks low and reselling them high have been devised since the Rothschilds demonstrated dramatically how profitable it could be. In recent years professional money managers by the dozens—and graduate students by the thousands—with access to computers have been inputting screens and stops and qualifying standards of every type and in just about every combination to test out possible buy-low, sell-high systems that work, at least on the computer. The fact that they're still at it indicates both that the goal is desirable and that it is yet to be attained.

The Depressed-Issues Strategy

One of those making an effort to formalize the theory of buy low, sell high in a viable manner is a successful marketing man—initials M.S.S.—with a background in mathematics. Here's how he describes his "Depressed-Issues Strategy."

"The buy-low approach endeavors to pick up companies that have a depressed market price but are fundamentally sound. The hope is that the reason for the depressed condition will be corrected within a short period of time and thus make the stock price rise. Perhaps one way to do this is to search out stocks that have had a wide range in their recent performance and are currently in the lower quartile of this range . . . another might be stocks that are selling at a low 'multiplier' . . . another might be companies that dropped in earnings from the previous year . . . another might be companies that lost money in the previous year.

"The second part of the strategy (or scheme or system) calls for the selection of a relatively large number of stocks, ten or more. Here, statistical theory comes into play. You can't, with any degree of certainty, forecast a rise of a specific percent for the market value of one stock. As the number of companies increases, you will approximate the total performance of the group. The results, obviously, will neither be equal to the best in the group nor will they be the poorest . . . they will be average. If the group is rising as a whole the average should outperform the market."

There are three criteria for issue selection:

1. *Wide price range*—a ratio of high to low of near 2:1

2. *Selling near low*—current price in lower 25 percent of the range

3. *Sound fundamentals*—reasonably good earnings, healthy financial situation, and attractive potential.

Below are a dozen diversified "depressed issues" culled by M.S.S. for investment in April, 1969:

Company	Recent high	Recent low	Price as of 4/14/69
City Investing	40⅞	18⅞	28¾
Dennison Mfg.	80	41¾	48⅝
Freeport Sulphur	77¾	32	33⅜
General Instrument	63¼	26	31
Global Marine	63⅜	27	27⅜
Harcourt Brace	105½	54½	63½
Murphy (G. W.)	42¼	17¾	18½
Perfect Film & Chem.	88½	35⅛	41
Products Research	47	23⅞	27¼
Sangamo Electric	62¼	27½	33⅞
Santa Fe Int'l. Co.	54¾	27½	31⅜
United Airlines	66½	34	40

Why were these issues down? A merger proposal that fell flat? A management change-over? Losses due to strikes? An industry price war? A nonrecurring type of misfortune? To separate the chronically depressed from the acute, M.S.S. studied the fundamentals; and to get a feel of the timing, he reviewed the technical factors, including a tabulation designed to give him "an isolated view in a fixed market environment in order to point up volume-price imbalances as well as levels of interest."

A glance at the quotations in your newspaper will tell you that as yet the Depressed-Issues Strategy has

not worked out with most of the dozen candidates for
early rebound listed above. Win, lose or break even,
however, M.S.S. ignores the "penny stocks" and screens
out the poorer risks while rummaging systematically
through the distress merchandise in the market for bargains. What's more, he does not kid himself into thinking that he is doing any more than paying his respects
as a mathematician to the power of numbers. And he is
perfectly aware that even after he has solved the first
part of the golden equation, buying low, he will still
have to figure out a system for selling high.

Everybody more or less understands that buy low*est*,
sell high*est* is an improbable proposition like a hole in
one, since nobody can possibly know that a low stock
won't go lower or a high stock higher. The game is to
come close. But most people who buy low price instead
of high value are bound to be disappointed in the stock
market, because they are dealing in junk. To make matters worse, some of the junk dealers have a habit of
letting their losses run on (they call this "sticking it
out"), because they are reluctant to admit a mistake.
And as their down-stock declines further they are prone
to buy more, rationalizing a purely emotional decision
as "averaging down."

Another habit of junk dealers who don't trust their
own judgment is to enter an order for their cheapie at a
limit well below the market price. By doing so they
are, in effect, betting against themselves. Because if
they are successful in obtaining the stock at *their* price,
that is, if it goes down to their limit, the chances are at
least 50–50 that it will continue to move in the same
direction. On the other hand, if their judgment of the

worth of the stock is correct and it goes straight up without first dropping down to their limit, they have botched their opportunity and lost the profit they might have made had they bought the stock at the market price.

There are shrewd investors (like Harold) who habitually buy depressed stocks of relatively good value and keep buying them on the way down, to put away until their potential is fully recognized by the market. But, too often, averaging down throws good money after bad, because gravity is a law that operates also in the stock market, and the sinker continues to sink of its own weight. On the other hand, Copeland, by averaging *up* on rising prices, is usually going in the right direction at the right time.

Every investor or speculator is essentially a bargain hunter. The more mature and gains-oriented is not concerned with low price, however, or the number of shares that his dollars will buy: he seeks the *most value for each dollar* of market price.

7

The
Sports

Teddy Bear is no more. And his species is dwindling in number and influence. Teddy Bear was a floor trader, one of the earlier breed of "my word is my bond," million-dollar shooters. But with the spread of "people's capitalism" and, concurrently, the growth of giant welfare and pension funds, foundations and billion-dollar mutual funds (to say nothing of those traditional institutional powerhouses, the banks and insurance companies), the floor trader's style has been cramped. The managers of commingled and tax-sheltered money have become too big and too many for the lone-hand sports like Teddy Bear.

Time was when with 10,000 or 20,000 shares Teddy could make a good thing all by himself. Nowadays it might have to be a relatively obscure or inactive stock

on a dull Friday afternoon in July for a solo operator
to make waves. And even then, by Monday's opening,
probably, a "technical correction" would be building up.
The educated hunch is not often a match anymore for
the creative computer. Center stage has been taken over
by the institutional money managers, the astute, young,
hard-nosed computer-assisted pros who (when the
game is going their way) enjoy two distinct advantages
over the Teddy Bears: lots more money and lots more
objectivity, because the money at stake is not their own.

Even dollar for dollar, young Joe Gogo, calling the
shots for a sprouting growth fund or a national union
retirement fund, enjoys better odds than the Teddy
Bears. However performance-oriented, Joe Gogo is essentially an investor seeking a specified-or-better return on capital, while the Teddy Bears are out-and-
out irreversible and incorrigible moon shooters. Joe
Gogo has a single, uncomplicated objective: money.
But for Teddy Bear, who also measured success by
profit, the dollars, as such, were merely token or symbol,
an acceptable receipt, for something else, a higher,
farther sort of goal that beckoned continually. Joe Gogo
takes his gains wherever he or his computer print-out
finds them. Other things being equal, Teddy preferred
to match wits with and beat his peers, the members of
the club, his fellow floor traders.

Teddy had the vision and reflexes of a speculator with
the soul (that old-fashioned word is peculiarly fitting)
of a sentimental sport—a split personality, if you like.
Head and heart were not always on the same beam.
Speculation, by definition as well as derivation, means
to spy out, to look ahead; and so, by application, the
speculator is one who puts his money where his vision
is. A venturesome opportunist, the speculator serves a

useful purpose, in economic theory at any rate, by helping to keep the law of supply and demand functioning.
By assuming relatively high risk, he supposedly makes
the market run more smoothly, taking up the slack or
adding to the supply of stock when it seems profitable
to do so. The difference between the speculator and the
investor in the financial sense is in the risk-reward
range, the speculator taking bigger risks at longer odds
in anticipation of larger rewards. Between the speculator and the sport, however, the difference is essentially
one of style or spirit, which can be dramatic, even tragic.

Teddy Bear was a gentleman—another old-fashioned
word. Although he's been gone for some years now, a
suicide at forty-four, his gentlemanly qualities are still
recalled at the luncheon club of the New York Stock
Exchange, where someone is almost certain to pay him
the ultimate compliment: "There weren't many like
him even in his time."

Unlike the majority of Stock Exchange members,
Teddy owned his own seat and traded strictly for his
own account. Although he had a tiny office on Broad
Street, it was not open to the public and his only client
was himself. His trades, while relatively few and far between, always involved sizable blocks. He appeared on
the floor every morning at ten o'clock and he rarely left
before the closing bell. He seemed to love it, and he
made friends as well as money. For one thing, he was
an unusually thoughtful, considerate human being. For
another, he was pleasant company, genial, mild tem-
pered and soft spoken, but more interested in listening
than in talking. A bachelor, he knew his way around
town. While he liked the ladies—and they liked him—
he was never reported to be serious about any particular

one. His parties were memorable, for although Teddy tended to get dimmed down and diminished in a crowd —out-pushed and out-louded—he came into his own as a host. His dinners gained him a reputation as a gourmet. But his secret was in the attention he lavished on his guests. He could be at one and the same time— another split in personality, apparently—a gentle, diffident supernumerary and an elegant showboat.

Breeding, evident in Teddy's manners, concealed the powerful drive underneath. Although his father was the senior partner of a prestigious investment banking house with century-old roots in a merchant banking firm in London, and a place was ready and waiting for Teddy when he took his degree from the Wharton School, he did not stay on the clear, straight road that was mapped out for him. Within three years Teddy was admitted to partnership. All he had to do, it seemed, was to follow orders and keep learning, and one day he would be sitting in his father's six-window corner office, running the whole operation; but Teddy chose to go off on his own. Resigning his partnership at the age of twenty-seven, he bought a seat on the Exchange and went onto the floor to trade strictly by and for himself. He continued to dine with his family in their Park Avenue co-op whenever he was free and to spend a week of his vacation with them every year, sometimes abroad, sometimes in their country house in Connecticut or their beach house in East Hampton; but he never asked his father's advice or initiated any business discussion with him.

If there was a single character trait that explained Teddy's market approach, it was determination to beat the system. (He had already beaten the system of nepotism in his father's firm by breaking away; and he was beating the marital system—his mother had been notoriously unfaithful to his father—by remaining unattached.) And every day on the floor of the Exchange he was trying to beat the Wall Street system by guessing how the other traders and the public would react to the failure of an international monetary conference that had not yet taken place, or to the conclusion of a merger deal under review by the Justice Department, and then, if he saw a worthwhile opportunity, going out on a limb with his own money.

As suggested, Teddy was a loner, not a leader, a soloist, though a quiet one, who could play along with or even support the chorus but could not comfortably be a member of it. He made generous contributions to cultural activities. He lent his name to fund-raising campaigns. He seemed like such a model citizen that even those who knew him well still expected him to find a "nice girl," marry, and settle down to a model, conventional way of life; and they hoped it would happen soon. But Teddy was totally preoccupied with beating the system.

Teddy's preoccupation was so intense that it found insufficient outlet on the trading floor five days a week, forty-eight weeks of the year. He spent the greater part of his annual vacation at the casino in Beaulieu or in Monte Carlo. And almost every Friday afternoon, as soon as the market was over, Teddy and one or two other traders of similar bent would share a limousine to the airport, already ticketed on the first flight for Las Vegas. There, each man for himself and still in competition with one another, they would attempt to beat a system that they did not understand nearly as well as the stock market and where the odds against them were even longer.

Though unrelated to any financial activities, Teddy's death was all of a piece with his life, part of the same pattern. Learning that he was suffering from leukemia and his time was limited, he took the final solution into his own hands. To the end he was thoughtful and considerate—and out to beat the system.

A successful, sporting speculator during the week, a losing gambler on Saturdays, Sundays and holidays. Two different men? Or two aspects of the same man?

The cab driver plunking down the hard-saved cost of his son's tuition to buy shares of a stock "given" him by a fare picked up on Wall Street is not a speculator but a gambler, because what he "spies out" is an illusion induced by the astigmatism of wishful thinking; and in any case he can't afford the risk of being wrong. All he's got to go by is his desire to beat the system of trying to hack out a living on the city streets. The principle, if we can call it that, is exactly the same for a manufacturer earning ten times as much who will go into hock on a new issue of an unseasoned, unlisted company because of a tip "given" him by a cab driver. He is a gambler acting not from objective observation but subjectively; he seeks an emotional outlet. For adventure? Or to beat the system by which he lives? Winning means something more to him than more money; losing means more than less money.

The gambler in the stock market poses at least one paradox. Why are so many people—middle and upper income brackets included—desperate to beat the system? What has persuaded millions of men and women that hard work and ability cannot make—or keep—their fortune? The continuing combination of higher taxes and lower buying power for the after-tax dollar serves to promote the capital gain as the quickest, surest way to get a leg up. A modest investment, or a modestly growing investment, won't do it, however, not in six months and one day. A capital gain of $1,000 or even $10,000, after taxes, may not be such a big deal. Conversely, loss of $1,000 or even $10,000, before taxes, may not be a catastrophe. So why not shoot the works, try for a jackpot, spectacular money, enough to break the bonds of financial or psychological frustration?

The nut of the paradox is that while amateur gamblers and sports heat up the market periodically by outbidding one another on already overpriced issues, conspicuously oils and mining stocks in the under-$5 range, the apparatus of the market is dedicated to the protection of widows and orphans and geared to the pace of the long-term investor. Naturally, the brokers and officials of the exchanges and regulatory bodies, voluntary or statutory, are aware of where the action is and what the consequences might be. They do what they can to police their marketplaces, to guarantee fair weights and measures, in effect. But the listed stock markets are auction markets, by and large, where prices are determined by buyers and sellers. And securities analysis is limited, necessarily, to the analyzable, a category that does not extend to many of the go-for-broke unlisted issues. So in spite of what the industry and its regulators might like, those customers who swing on pipe dreams and moon shots simply will not buy stocks as investments or approach the stock market with the same rational attitude they presumably show when considering life insurance or a financial decision in their own business.

A typical amateur sport is Shoot-the-Works Sherman. Like Teddy Bear, Sherman would be regarded as a very nice guy, although there the resemblance begins and ends. Sherman is now in his fifties, married (for the third time), father of four (two with each of his previous wives), salaried and in debt. Alimony, support, and the desire to see his children well educated cost more than Sherman earns. His current wife, Wendy, works to buy her own clothes, which helps but not enough. Sherman would like very much to do nice things for Wendy, to make her happy and proud of him. Since lottery tickets do not happen to be the in thing in Sherman's set, he buys stocks with an eye to winning the Super Grand De Luxe Prize every time. For Sherman an investment decision is an act of desperation; it is also a fearful, fervent, religious sacrifice.

Sherman has an important middle-management job as advertising-promotion director of one of the bigger book clubs. But this is as far as he's likely to go, because of the time and energy he expends on trying to strike it rich. As he sees it, he is trapped: by concentrating on his job and gaining another rung on the corporate ladder, he might add $10,000 a year to his salary, not enough after taxes to make an appreciable difference in his circumstances; and on the other hand, by concentrating more on making money for himself in the stock market, he runs the risk of being passed up for promotion, as has already happened once.

Strangely and perhaps significantly, Sherman seems rather choosy about how he will strike it rich. Though all his available cash and credit go into stocks that he hopes will make him independent financially, not just any vehicle will do. For instance, when he was made a vice president of his company, Sherman became eligible to participate in an executive stock-option plan. Despite the fact that the company stock appreciated about 35 percent during his option period, Sherman picked up only 300 (of 1,000) shares, and even so, only to demonstrate loyalty. He could not bring himself to divert more funds from his potential doublers for the sake of an assured additional profit of a few thousand dollars. For him, a bird in the hand is not worth two in the bush.

Sherman, who is a bright conversationalist, delights in beguiling his listeners with an endless Sunday night serial of fresh-but-familiar bonanza dreams. Investment ideas are no problem for Sherman. In addition to his broker—an ex-brother-in-law whom he would like to leave but won't out of regard for the ex-wife concerned—friends, associates, his boot-black and his barber, other sources are systematically cultivated by Sherman. He answers every coupon ad in the *Times* financial section and in the *Wall Street Journal* that offers free investment information, in the expectation of being contacted by eager young brokers from whom he might extract new and exciting ideas. And when he is contacted, the conversation, over the phone, generally goes something like this:

EAGER YOUNG BROKER. You sent in for our research write-up on Honeywell. Are you interested in the stock?

SHERMAN.   In a way, sort of. What else do you like, I mean *really* like?

EAGER YOUNG BROKER. Well, sir, that would depend on your objective.

SHERMAN. My objective? To make money! What else does anyone go into the stock market for?

EAGER YOUNG BROKER. Yes, sir. But how much money are you looking for, if I may ask? And how quick? And how much risk can you afford to take? What are your resources and your obligations? That's what I mean, sir, by your objective.

SHERMAN. My obligations and my resources are my own business. All I'm asking you for is a good stock, which is supposed to be your business.

EAGER YOUNG BROKER. I'm sorry, sir. I was trying to get to know more about you so I could offer an idea or two that would be suitable for you.

SHERMAN. Look, as far as I'm concerned, what's suitable is a stock that will make money—lots of it and quickly. You find the stock and I'll take care of the rest.

Earnings, dividends, estimated sales, were unimportant to Sherman. Price and current market action and the promise of an early run-up were the main considerations. The more obscure the stock the better, for Sherman did not shy from the role of "discoverer." When an eager young broker did come up with an idea that struck his fancy, Sherman made the purchase through his ex-brother-in-law.

In one instance, told about a suitably obscure stock listed on the American Exchange that had run up from 5½ to 12 in a matter of weeks, Sherman began to ask questions. The young broker did not have the answers but offered to find out all he could. His research department could not help him, however; the information

requested was not available. Whereupon the young
broker persuaded the analyst who was responsible for
following that particular industry to make a field trip
for the purpose of researching and evaluating the company. The analyst did his job thoroughly and con-
scientiously, summarizing in a four-page report his
appraisal of the company's management, product, distribution and advertising, as well as the usual financial
data, explaining the recent market action in the stock,
and concluding that it might be "an interesting speculation for high-risk accounts." Now very excited, the
young broker phoned Sherman to read him the analyst's
report. Sherman was surprised, impressed and pleased
with the service but disinclined to hear the details.
Disappointed but assuming that Sherman was busy at
the moment, the broker offered to mail the report.
Sherman told him not to bother, and, thanking him
abruptly, hung up so that he would lose no more
precious time in placing the order with his ex-brother-
in-law.

Apart from the question of which broker got the
commission, how can we interpret Sherman's refusal to
read—or even listen to—a fresh appraisal by a trained
analyst about a company in whose stock he was contemplating putting a substantial amount of money?
Was he afraid of being confused by the facts? Or like
many gamblers, was he already preparing an out for
himself? If he read the report, acted on it, and his actions turned out to be wrong, then his judgment might
be criticized. But on the other hand, if he didn't know
what the analyst had reported and acted solely on the
basis of the original tip, and then if the stock turned
sour, Sherman could put the blame on the original

tipster! Rather than risk full responsibility for a mistake—or share any of the credit for a success—he preferred to buy in the blind.

Buying in the blind and having a desperate need for
a lot of money with which to break out of financial
bonds are two of the characteristics common to many
market sports.

What makes Sherman shoot the works at the sound
of a high flier? For one thing, pessimism about earning
enough money at his job to fulfill both his obligations
and his desires. For another thing, pride, a need to be
different, to do something spectacular on his own, to
show his wife and his two ex-wives and his four children, along with his friends, neighbors and associates,
that he is capable of independent, even contrary, action; that while lesser men must grind out their first
downs three and four yards at a time, he, Sherman,
can score with the daring bomb! Spiritually, a dropout;
socially, he is very competitive.

There are many Shermans in the market, well-edu-
cated professional and managerial-class men and
women who no longer look to their own business or
profession as the highway to financial success. They
hope to beat both the economic and the social system,
along with the double-squeeze of taxes and inflation,
through margin and capital gains. They are individualists, in some cases exhibitionists under wraps, in a
society where most people are required to work in
concert, as members of a team, for a long time after
they have proven their ability to lead the band or to
call the plays for others. In the meantime these sports
feel compelled to demonstrate to their dependents, to

their detractors, to themselves and to the indifferent rest-of-the-world that they can get to the top, front and center, through their own devices.

Another trait shared by a surprising number of sports is finickiness about the "sure things," or "locks," they will back. Teddy Bear wouldn't accept a lock on one of the top spots in Wall Street, his father's job. Instead he insisted on pitting his brains and nerve against that of the pros, the toughest, shrewdest traders on the floor. Sherman too in a favored position had chosen not to take advantage of it. He could have made a respectable sum of money—enough to alleviate immediate needs—by picking up all the options he held in the shares of his own company. It was a sure thing. But to finance it, Sherman would have had to sell some of his pipe-dream stocks, and this he refused to do.

Teddy Bear was a success by any dollar standard even if he did not succeed in beating the system at Las Vegas. Sherman, with similar drives, will probably fail, because Wall Street is to him what Las Vegas was to Teddy—an unfamiliar, alien system. Obviously, it should be easier to beat a system you know; and to the extent that you go afield for esoteric systems to beat you are really seeking to beat yourself.

But, you say, you have personal knowledge of Shermans who have shot the works and tripled their money in a year, quadrupled it in two years. No doubt. It happens in every strong bull market. On a rising tide some stocks may rise spectacularly. And the lucky shareowner, if he buys and sells at the right time, holds the winning sweepstakes ticket. Of course, when the market changes direction, as it does and must, the highest fliers have the farthest to fall.

Can the gambler-speculator-sport succeed or fail on

his own, or does the market make the decision? In other words, how much of the end result is determined by personal qualities, such as foresight, courage and tenacity, as well as financial resources?

It's a little like a girl paddling a canoe downriver. As long as the current is going her way she may think she's a pretty hot canoeist. But when the current changes direction—or she does—it becomes immediately apparent just how good she really is.

8

The

Serendipity Kids

Among a number of qualified observers who were asked to account for the most successful investors in their personal experience was Professor A. J. Briloff, a practicing C.P.A., teacher and writer. Briloff cited three individuals as "most successful psychically as well as financially." All three lived in the Rochester, New York, area, singularly enough, although in no way related to one another. Over the years each of the three had concentrated their investments in Eastman Kodak and Xerox (the latter when it was still known as Haloid), either as an expression of community pride or because the local companies were more familiar to them than any others. By chance or by sagacity each had found rewards far beyond anything sought or hoped for.

This is serendipity in the stock market.

Some have it and some do not, apparently. Serendipity may be as much a matter of choice as of chance. While Rochester is a prosperous city, obviously not everyone in the area is investment-rich; not everyone had what it took in the way of judgment, character, personal style and community spirit to put their savings into two local companies with such odd made-up names as Kodak and Xerox. Just as by no means have all the potential investors in Cambridge, Massachusetts, had the luck or wisdom or local pride to put their faith and their money into something called Polaroid.

Those of us who have to search and study and deliberate for our quota of stock market successes find it difficult to comprehend how winners can *just happen* to some people. Or perhaps it's not so much incomprehension as envy. We might not mind being dumb-lucky too, incapable of distinguishing between good and poor, if we could be sure we would come out better in the end. An item in *The Wall Street Journal* might remind us of a favorite soup, and instead of making a note to buy two family-size cans at the supermarket on the way home we would have the happy inspiration immediately to buy 200 shares of stock in the company. Eureka!

Why wrack your brains weighing facts, why struggle with decisions? Luck will outbeat science, as they say, any day of the week. Hasn't everyone heard of the little old lady whose conscientious broker phoned to advise her that a certain stock in her portfolio should be sold because from all signs it was due for a fall? But the little old lady, who had been holding the stock for a long, long time and who liked the company's products well enough to use them exclusively, didn't want to hurt the company's feelings by showing disloyalty, especially at a time when the company was evidently in distress, so she chose to hold. The stock slipped and fell and slipped some more, just as the broker had predicted, but still the little old lady held. She felt embattled but would not surrender as long as the company didn't. And then one day there was a tender offer for the depressed stock of the fine old company, and then a second tender offer, and then a third. As a three-way fight for control developed, the stock began to bounce up a point or two a session and then to vault up four or five points a day. When the price topped the all-time high and seemingly could go no higher, the little old lady decided that the company didn't need her support any longer, so she sold her stock. The virtues of loyalty and perseverance were rewarded with a whopping big capital gain!

This is the sort of manna from heaven that is less apt to fall to husbands than to wives—at least, in my family. Marguerite has long held Simplicity Patterns in high regard as a company. In early 1968, with no one actively recommending the issue to her, Marguerite suddenly latched on to the idea for reasons unrelated to the market. Nine months later her stock was worth twice as much as she had paid for it. A lucky shot in the dark? Also on her own advice, because she liked the product, she bought shares in Villager Industries, the same year. This time she did not quite double her money; from March through November the stock appreciated about 80 percent. One more example of Marguerite in Serendip. Because the people at her bank branch had been exceptionally nice to her about overdrafts and the like, she bought the stock. And *it* appreciated over 50 percent in 1968. While not all of Marguerite's inspirations have turned out quite so hap-

pily, her S.Q. (Serendipity Quotient) is high enough
to impress anyone but a C.F.A. (Chartered Financial
Analyst).

The most memorable serendipitist of my acquaintance was a lady broker named Sara. Sara was in her
sixties, a five-time grandmother when she went into
the securities business, apparently because of somebody's remark in passing that she had a good head for
figures. In just two years Sara had developed a substantial clientele, largely by giving talks at investment
seminars for invited audiences. Even after she was well
established, Sara continued to participate in her firm's
investment seminars, partly because she found new
faces stimulating and partly because she was so well
received, but mainly because she enjoyed talking without interruption. In recent years Sara had taken to using
a hearing aid, which she loved because it enabled her to
turn off questions or arguments or competition for attention. A short, round person, Sara dressed invariably
in conservatively tailored navy blue suits, but a sweet
face, pink cheeks and perpetually smiling rosebud lips
made her unforgettably appealing to look at. Some of
her fellow brokers uncharitably attributed the happy
smile to the fact that Sara's turned-off (except when
she was talking) hearing aid spared her the effort of
coping with the inanities that passed for conversation
most of the time in a boardroom.

It was Sara's conviction that anything that could be
understood could be explained. And she was exceptionally good at explaining investment techniques and
strategy to her listeners. At one seminar that I happened to attend, after she had first captivated and then
enchanted a large audience, she was asked where she
got her investment ideas. Sara's sweet smile seemed to

sweeten further, a sign that she was pleased with the
question, and she replied that whenever her own financial insight was temporarily dimmed and her research department could not help her, she just walked
out of the office and into the street. And there she always "stepped right into it"—the right idea at the right
time. Without fail. A Chrysler station wagon might be
parked at the curb and Sara would suddenly recall all
the leverage in the company's capitalization. "Aha!" she
would tell herself. "Chrysler! What a bargain in this
market!" Or, crossing the street, she would be almost,
but not quite, splashed by a bakery truck. And Sara,
drawing back in the nick of time, would exclaim to herself, "Aha! Continental Baking! Children have to eat
in any kind of market, in every kind of economy. So
what could be better at a dopey time like this than a
nice defensive stock, a nice respectable food company?"
Or maybe on a slow day for Sara she might have to
walk all the way to the corner before she would notice
the Lucky Strike billboard and remark to herself, "Aha!
American Tobacco! The cancer scare's scared them into
diversifying their interests. Dividends good, growth not
bad, what could be so wrong?" Or she would see a
tourist carrying a camera, any camera, and it would
come to her, "Aha! Who is Polaroid making rich—besides Polaroid? *Kodak!* Let Polaroid sell the Swingers
and have the crazy P/E ratio. Who makes and sells
most of the film? *Kodak!* And who sells Polaroid their
color negatives? *Kodak!* So who is Polaroid working for?
Right! And look at the difference in the P/E!"

When she had finished answering the question, Sara's
eyes were smiling as sweetly as her lips. The message
was implicit. Every broker could read the numbers, and
every broker had a research department that was com-

petent at supplying the numbers. But Sara had a little
something extra, a sixth sense, or the great good fortune
to be in the right place to receive the good ideas when
they came down from above. It was the kind of bounty
possessed only by the sweetest, purest, most innocent
of grandmothers—or so it seemed, watching little,
round Sara being surrounded at the conclusion of the
program by the ladies and gentlemen of the audience.

As I was leaving, one of Sara's fellow seminarians, a
seasoned, highly competent broker named Leo, caught
my elbow. "They're always like this," said Leo. "She's
the one they want to see when it's over. She's the most
phenomenal person in the business, so charming, so
ladylike, so inspired, so . . . so . . . !" he sputtered.

"She's a fine speaker, isn't she?"

Leo nodded. "A better talker than a listener. But
who's got as much to say as Sara or can say it so
nicely?"

"Tell the truth, Leo, you believe everything she said?
Like this business of doing her research on the street?"

"It's true." Leo shrugged, an expression of regret
settling over his features. "Me, if I went outside looking
for an idea, I'd step into it, too," he replied, an edge in
his voice, "a pile of you-know-what!"

Sara was the envy and despair of her fellow brokers,
but they respected the results she achieved. For all her
grandmotherly put-ons, she was no charlatan, no faker
or phony. Call it chance or inspiration or a relaxed
mind or whatever you choose, she was one of the blessed
ones to whom good things came when they were
needed.

Most investors, like most brokers, have to work hard
for their rewards, studying any number of likely companies before they can discover one of relatively su-

perior value. As with other worthwhile things, investment success seems to be a product of 90 percent per-
spiration and 10 percent inspiration, although 90 percent of the investors usually act as if they were 100
percent possessed of the 10 percent ingredient. Whether
it derives from choice or chance, one thing is for sure,
serendipity is only to be found on the side of the
winners.

9

The
Smarts

The desire to excel, to stand out and be admired or envied, is no less human in the stock market than elsewhere. One might go so far as to say with Lord Lyttelton, *"Where none admire, 'tis useless to excel."* Nevertheless, there may be a high tax to pay in the pursuit of admiration for its own sweet sake rather than as a by-reward for excellence.

Most investors and speculators desire to excel at making money. For some, however, the monetary consideration may be secondary to the emotional; and so it is with the Smarts.

A sophisticated investor or speculator employs any and all techniques of the market that can lead to larger profits or smaller losses. A Smart uses sophisticated techniques as a matter of habit or preference even when simple, basic approaches might be more effective.

Who are the Smarts? What are they doing in the market? And how much are they getting out of it?

There are Smarts for whom the investment of capital offers additional opportunities to practice social one-upmanship.

At the other extreme there are Smarts with social, physical or psychic handicaps, hypersensitive people who hope to strike a balance with fate or nature or their ancestry or fellow man by using the market as billy or crutch.

In between there are Smarts who are egoists eager to persuade themselves of their own superiority. There are also quite a few incorrigible competitors for whom the market represents a game in which the goal is to outdo or outshine all other participants. And some are showboats so intent on dazzling those around them with the brilliance of their performance that they may magnify gains and minimize losses to achieve the desired impression.

Smarts are such an ancient, virile and ubiquitous clan that there is a drop or two of Smart blood in many investors and more than a drop in most speculators.

Anyone, in fact, can be tempted to act like a Smart sometimes.

A he-man type star of stage and screen who in private life is an uncommonly domesticated husband and responsible citizen, quite bland in personality, gets bored with himself every once in a while and tries to impress his wife, children and broker with the notion that he is not merely a celluloid tiger. Whenever the antipassive virus invades his bloodstream, the actor turns Smart and calls his broker. "You know Don

Doakes [another star]? Don's broker put him in options, puts and calls. He's doing so great, he's bragging
about it." The broker, who is used to hearing clients
count their friends' profits instead of their own, invariably replies by asking, "And how are you doing?"
The actor does an aural doubletake, as if he has been
thrown the wrong cue, "Me? Fine, *but* . . ."

Another client of the same broker, a normally prag-
matic businessman with a wholehearted appreciation
of capital gains, holds a portfolio of quality stocks that
give him very little cause for complaint. But periodically he is thrown off stride by some of his swinging
associates, Smarts who count all their winners out loud,
their biggest winners loudest. Then, beginning to feel
cowed, the investor informs his broker that "everybody
else" is making greater gains than he is. He would like
to have something "interesting" to match. The broker
replies, "Just add up your holdings this month and see
what you're worth compared to last month. Then go
ahead and match your friends—not winners, but profits."

When money is being made, Smarts tend to adopt
the more spectacular moneymakers for their own. Nobody hears about their spectacular losers except their
broker, and he won't tell.

Another market manner of Smarts is mobility,
switching from broker to broker or from investment
adviser to investment adviser, always from the less
chichi to the more so. Similarly, Smarts may flit from
one stock to another, "to keep out of the crowd," as
they say, "because the little fellow is always wrong." If
in the process they suffer losses, Smarts may be consoled by the thought that "the little fellow" is bound to
be hurt worse.

While Smarts ordinarily shun a "popular" issue, they

will welcome the opportunity to be "the first one" in or out of any stock.

With a larger order, say for 1,000 or 2,000 shares, a Smart makes a practice of trying to fox his broker. Instead of disclosing the full size of his order so that the office broker can enlist the experience and on-the-spot judgment of the firm's floor broker, the Smart masterminds the transaction by going in 100 or 200 shares at a time. His ostensible reason is that he does not wish to "disturb the market" and, possibly, have the price get away from him. But often that is just what does happen. On the second—certainly by the third—100- or 200-share order for the same stock from the same source, the floor broker knows that he has been kidded along; not only that, but the other floor brokers at the trading post, as well as the specialist, have caught on to the ploy and will take advantage of the knowledge if they can on behalf of their own clients. In such circumstances Smart may outwit himself. He will get a better price, usually, by giving his office broker a "not held" order for the full amount, enabling the floor broker to use his judgment and feel of the market at the trading post to obtain the best possible execution.

A broker can identify a Smart over the telephone by his withholding of pertinent information or by the utilization of an intricate technique when the direct approach might be more advantageous, or by the expression of attitudes such as these:

SMART.   What do you like today?
BROKER.   For long-term appreciation? Johns-Manville.
SMART.   What's the big deal? I can get *that* from any broker in town.

Or:

SMART. I just got a stock you never heard of. What do you think of Sodawater Pipeline?

BROKER. Never heard of it.

SMART. See! I hear it's going to 50.

BROKER. I'll find out all I can from research and let you know.

SMART. Research? Then everybody on the street will know. Buy me 100 now—at a limit two points under the market—and don't tell anybody!

The "limit" is a giveaway that Smart doesn't want to buy the stock as much as he wants to impress his broker. Because if the stock is really running up to 50, as Smart says, the odds are against its pausing to drop two points at this particular price level in order to accommodate Smart's limit order. On the other hand, if Smart does want the stock, he is taking an unnecessary risk, because a simple market order will get it for him right now.

But Smarts don't use market orders if they can help it. They favor cop-outs like limits; and "day orders," which expire if not executed by the end of the trading day on which they are entered; or "fill or kill" orders, which are canceled if not executed in their entirety as soon as represented at the trading post by the floor broker; and other now-you-see-it-now-you-don't trading devices.

When a will-o'-the-wisp order goes unexecuted, Smart likes to tell everybody about it with never a hint that perhaps he entered an unfillable order. In his stories, "somebody had a corner on the market"; or "my broker matched and lost" (meaning that there was another simultaneous bid on the trading floor, and each bid was at least equal to the amount of stock offered, so the two floor brokers concerned flipped a coin to decide the buyer and, naturally, Smart's dumb broker lost); or "there was stock ahead" (meaning that there were other orders at the same price in the specialist's book with priority over Smart's); or "the market was thin" (meaning that there were no sellers at the time); and so forth, always dramatically.

Even if Smart fully intends to complete a transaction, he cannot refrain from doing a buck and wing when a straightforward step might get him to his goal more swiftly and surely. Sometimes, instead of the common stock he wants in his portfolio, Smart buys convertible bonds that could under certain conditions be exchanged for the stock; or he buys a call and pays a premium for an option to buy the stock eventually at a fixed price within a fixed time, although not at today's price today. Or he gets "the taste" of owning the stock and still satisfies his craving to demonstrate sophistication by trading in the warrants of the particular security. Or he arbitrages, trying to capitalize on any difference in price for the same issue between, say, the New York Stock Exchange and the Pacific Coast Stock Exchange, by purchasing the stock in one market and simultaneously selling it in the other, hoping to make a profit on the differential.

A fairly unusual Smart, though rapidly becoming less so, is Junior. A graduate student at an eastern university and barely old enough to have a brokerage account, this particular Junior tries to show up his father by outsmarting and outperforming him in the market. Whatever stock Senior buys, Junior sells short; and when Senior sells, Junior buys a call on the same stock. It's as though Senior were rolling dice and Junior betting he was wrong on each roll. Once, learning that he and his father held the same stock, Junior wrote a straddle; that is, he bought both a put and a call on the stock, meaning that he agreed to deliver his 100 shares or to accept 100 more if the stock moved enough either way to cause one of the options to be exercised. For the price of the premiums Junior practically guaranteed that he would be able to top his father. Practically but not quite. On that occasion the stock remained relatively flat during the option period.

Junior has taken courses in corporate finance, stock market fundamentals, and investment strategy. But the idea of just buying or selling a stock outright, the way it is mostly done by millions of the older generation, he considers greasy kid stuff. His kicks come from using his own capital to cock a snook at his father and his father's "smug, established, settled-down crowd."

How does he do? This particular young Smart is both erratic and bright. While his average of right to wrong is no better than 50–50 overall, his rights have been big enough to keep him comfortably in the black. But he is still frustrated, because during the same period his square father, plodding along on old-fashioned fundamentals, has steadily outperformed him in rate of return on invested capital.

Smarts, young and old, tend to go in for charting. They regard themselves—or wish to be regarded—as advanced students of timing. After all, they point out, there are three ingredients in a successful transaction: the right security, the right price and the right time. Of the three, the last is the most difficult to determine, and the most crucial. Obviously, you can have a good stock at a fair price—there are hundreds of these to be had—but if it is not about to move during the term of your investment objective, it's not much good to you.

Consequently, the conversation of charting Smarts is spiced with references to such tools as the advance-decline line, the advance-decline oscillator, moving averages, odd-lot balance index, mutual fund liquidity ratio, short interest, on-balance volume, tick volume, negative on-balance volume, and line charts versus point and figure charts, as well as such analytical terms as support, resistance, uptrend channels and downtrend channels.

Chartists believe that there are recurrent and discernible patterns in stock prices and trading volume from which trends can be predicted. The study of timing is a valid and valuable activity, of course. And technical analysis, of which charting is one method, may be an aid in securities selection as well as in the timing of purchases and sales, when used along with fundamental research. The mistake of chart bugs is to expect too much of *auxiliary* tools or to believe that theories that have never been fully tested can give them a shortcut to success.

To most professionals, technical analysis is twentieth-century haruspication using charts instead of chicken entrails. To Smarts, however, the chart may represent a form of market diploma attesting visibly and tangibly to superior trading literacy.

In 1967 and 1968 many Smarts were attracted to the hedge funds, partly because of their strong performance at that time but also because it was widely known that few hedge funds accepted participation for less than $100,000, and many required as much as $1,000,000. The not-so-rich Smarts hoped their friends and neighbors would put them in the million-dollar-minimum class.

It should go without saying that the investment

media and strategies favored by Smarts are all there to
be used for risk-reducing or money-making purposes.
The media—securities options, convertible bonds, warrants, rights, etc.—can't be blamed for their misappli-
cation by some investors. The same is true for the type
of order entered—limits, stop loss, fill or kill, all or
none, day orders, etc.; each serves a useful purpose
when intelligently employed. There is an appropriate
medium or technique or strategy for every legitimate
trading purpose. *Purpose is the point.* In the hands of a
purposeful, knowledgeable trader a complex approach
can be productive, while in the hands of a Smart it
may become esoteric, window dressing, form without
substance.

Smart is like a ball player who tries for a difficult
one-hand catch when two hands would be surer and
easier; or like a musician who is long on trills, cadenzas
and other embellishments but short on melody.

Comparing the purpose of an investment with the
function of the investment medium or technique is one
way to identify a Smart maneuver. But you don't always have to dig that deep. Sometimes you can spot a
Smart right off, by his groove.

In 1967 and 1968 the clues were loud and proud: "I
was in Polaroid at 22 and Xerox at 10 and IBM at 48.
Before the splits. Know what else? I've still got them.
But my broker said *I* was out of *my* mind when I told
him to pick up University Computing at 13!"

Since it is just as chic to match losers at certain
times, in 1969 a Smart monologue went something like
this: "Boy, when I crack up I crack up in the very best
company—like with Jimmy Ling, like with those Litton
whiz kids, like with that big whatsisname from National
General. And would you believe an offshore oil gusher

in reverse? That's me—in Zapata Norness at 59, out at 14!"

And sometimes it is more in to be out. By May 26, 1970, after the Dow-Jones Industrial Average had been shorn almost 36 percent, those Smarts who hadn't quit earlier were giving a good imitation of investors who had, yawning at market talk: if they never went back in it would be too soon. But within just four days— while the average was shooting up 79 points, 12.5 percent—well, market chic changes just as fast as any other.

Clearly, Smart is paying for an effect, hoping to project his personality through the superior or, at least, interesting performance of the securities that he buys or sells or associates with himself conversationally.

What, then, is the reckoning? How do Smarts stack up against true sophisticates and plain everyday investors? It is very difficult to be sure since their own testimony is suspect and results observed in individual cases vary enormously.

Inasmuch as a primary aim of the Smarts is respectful recognition, their capital assets may, in the deepest sense, be calculated in the currency of pride and envy, their net short- and long-term capital gains or losses expressed as plus or minus status symbols.

In purely financial terms, any estimate of their effectiveness would have to include an appraisal of two opposed factors: first, the negative impact of immature exhibitionism on market performance; second, the positive force of the drive to excel.

Logically, it might seem that, other things being equal, a Smart should do less well than an investor with both eyes focused on the profit goal. Like a motorist distracted by a long-legged girl in a micromini,

Smart should make slower progress and run more risk of mishap than those who are concentrating strictly on reaching their destination. But this is not always the case, not even the rule. Because to the extent that exhibitionism spurs him on to excel, to outdo, to outperform those around him, Smart may compensate for his handicaps and by sheer drive overcome his obstacles, self-erected or otherwise. As in any business or profession, *intensity* of purpose, the will to succeed, can offset a multitude of shortcomings.

How Smart makes out, in the final analysis, is determined largely by the outcome of the inner contest between the negative and positive aspects of the overweening vanity that motivates him. Like the rest of us, Smart usually gets something roughly like what he really wants and works for hard enough. In the long run anyway. And to the extent that he is working toward ephemeral goals he must expect to end up with nonfinancial rewards.

Or, as it is written in Genesis: *"Unstable as water, thou shalt not excel."*

10

The
Can't-Losers

After the market's close on the day of President Kennedy's assassination, a broker received a phone call from an elderly client who was in the hospital recuperating from a heart attack. Because of the patient's condition, he had not been allowed to read the newspapers, listen to the radio, or look at television. But because he was a worrier and accustomed to watching his investments closely, he had been given permission by his doctor to phone his broker once each afternoon to receive the closing quotes. On this tragic day, the conversation between the bedridden, uninformed client and the weary broker went as follows:

"Hello, Dan. Norman. How's ABC?"
"69½. Down 8."

"Oh! How's DEF?"

"112. Down 22."

"What? How's GHI?"

"13¼. Down 4."

"No! How's JKL?"

"167. Down 24⅛."

"Dan! Are these just *your* prices—or the same every-place?"

The story is true except for names and numbers. This particular investor couldn't see himself as a loser, couldn't imagine or accept a general market decline. At all times he had to keep bullish about everything with which he was associated. An extreme case, admittedly; but the can't-losers are all extremists.

Some of the greatest debacles in stock market history have been brought about not by speculators but by investors—nice guys, maybe, good to their families and loyal to their friends—who were caught up in a compulsive whirl of runaway hope and, when the tide turned against them, couldn't accept reality, wouldn't sell. Instead of backing out and taking a moderate loss, they went all the way down with their investments to a catastrophic crash.

Why?

Why will the same investor who buys readily, without undue hesitation, sell reluctantly if at all?

Why do some investors, women especially, feel that selling a stock that is ailing is being mean and heartless, like abandoning a handicapped child?

Why will an intelligent, otherwise rational investor stay, stay, stay with a dead issue, harboring only one ambition—to get even and then get out?

Since the answer does not lie in the investment, it

must derive from the investor, his personality, his character, his image of himself.

According to the psychologists, people who can't lose, who can't be wrong, whose confidence in themselves is shaken by a mistake or an error of judgment, are striving for omniscience, for a feeling of omnipotence. Two-dollar words aside, the can't-losers can't detach themselves, the inner core of their self-respect, from the consequences of their actions. They don't just buy stocks or bonds, they commit themselves. They purchase securities with their honor and self-esteem as well as with their money. When one of their selections falters, the failure is symptomatic, these investors feel. It is as though in making an investment decision they assume responsibility for the fortunes of the company, for the developments within the particular industry, for the mood of the market, and for the economy as a whole; and no matter what happens, they can't let go, they feel compelled to hang on, as an article of faith.

Can't-losers have heard the old refrain: "Cut your losses and let your profits run," and they do let their profits run, along with their losses. They regard a sale as a confession of failure.

The typical can't-loser tells himself, when one of his holdings has begun to slip, "Just a temporary fluctuation, maybe another point or two and it will turn around." The bullish face again. The broker may say, "If you think it's only going down another point or two, protect yourself, put in a stop loss order three points under the market. If you're right, there's no harm done. But if you're wrong, if it keeps going down, you're out of it with only a three point loss from where it's at now, and you're better off, too." But even if the can't-loser listens to his broker and puts in the stop loss

order, he won't stick to it. After his stock has gone down
two points, he moves his stop loss order down three.
Or he says, "Let's give it 10 percent. After all, when I
bought the stock, you told me there was a downside risk
of 10 percent. I accepted that then, I can't go back on it
now." Meanwhile, as the stock continues to sink and
the paper losses rise, the can't-loser is reading up on
the company, looking not for flaws or signs of weakness—oh no!—but for affirmative signs. And seeking, he
finds enough to justify his determination to wait out
the "temporary" condition.

Sometimes self-delusion is good medicine! Wasn't
it Pierre duPont who said, "There's more money made
by the seat of your pants than with your head"? He
was attesting to the virtue of patience, not stubbornness.
Still, when a failing stock begins to gain, the distinction
between stubbornness and patience fades in the mind of
the holder. Whatever it was that motivated him to stick
has been justified; he is not only happy but vindicated.
Now he may never sell that stock. Absolutely never. It
has endeared itself to him for life. He is beholden to it
for the restoration of his self-respect.

But in the event that hope should not suffice or that
reason should prevail and the can't-loser does sell a
stock on the way down, the resulting financial loss may
not be the worst or the last of it. The seller feels
shown up, exposed. His loyalty and patience have been
betrayed. Doubting himself now, he *hates* the offending
stock. He will never forgive it. If years later the company or industry should recover and the stock take off
again, he will not buy it, not even if there is reason to
believe that it will hit new highs. The can't-loser who
has sold a losing stock is like a woman who will not
remarry a man she has once divorced for infidelity; no

matter if he is reformed, she can't trust him and he's shaken her confidence in herself.

Can't-losers can feel almost as emotional about some stocks they have never owned. Having once considered investing in a stock and decided against it, they don't always drop it there. They read the quotes and watch the progress of the stock to confirm the wisdom of their negative decision. Should the stock rise appreciably, they feel awful about it, because, once more, their judgment has been exposed as faulty.

Should a broker re-recommend the passed-up stock, now rising on higher volume, soon perhaps to become a glamor stock, the answer is a flat No. A can't-loser cannot admit that he was wrong. He will never buy that stock, no matter how enthusiastically or authoritatively recommended. The stock has given offense by acting contrary to his original views. It has been excommunicated, as far as he is concerned, and he wishes it all the bad luck in the world. He will watch the daily quotations, however, always looking for the fatal turn for the worse, the retrogression regarded as inevitable. Only after a fall in price, even if the fluctuation is temporary, can the can't-loser give up reading the quotations.

Selling a winning stock may not be easy, either, for the habitual can't-loser. He will continue to keep an eye on the prices and watch for news of the company. If it turns out that he has sold short of the top by a wide margin, he is hurt, not so much because of the additional profit that might have been made—he knows that no one can catch every last point of a rise—but because of the emotional implications of what he now considers to be a premature sale. He may continue to follow the lost winner for months, applying mental body English to the reported prices. And not until the stock drops off to the level at which he sold it can he give up his vigil.

Not only investors but also speculators and even Wall Street professionals are guilty of emotionalism about their securities judgments, at least some of the time.

A broker who had recommended Raytheon almost a decade ago, just before Harold Geneen resigned the presidency and the company began to flounder, will not suggest the stock to any of his clients anymore—not even after the company began making notable progress and the stock was cited as a top buy by the broker's own research department.

Through the same kind of nonprofessional self-involvement another broker has developed a lasting peeve against a senior analyst in his own research department. About five years ago the broker heard the head of a freight forwarding company wax enthusiastic about the future of containerization in general and of McLean Industries in particular. Interested in the stock for himself as well as for his clients, the broker checked with his firm's transportation analyst who literally laughed out loud at the idea. "Containerization," the analyst said, "is a long way off. And McLean is . . . well, if you want to make money on McLean Industries, I'll tell you what you do. You find out from Malcolm McLean's P.R. man when he's going to make a speech. You buy the stock the day before he speaks, and you sell it the day after. He's a great personality and he makes a lot of speeches, so you'll get a lot of profitable trades out of it. But don't look for earnings on the books of McLean Industries, not for a helluva long time." The stock, which had been selling around 11, began almost immediately to run up and didn't stop until it hit the high 40's, while the broker suffered. Then the stock turned around and came right back down again. The analyst had not been correct but he was not fundamentally wrong, either. However, his advice was never again sought or taken by this broker, who, as a result, passed up a number of good ideas that might have compensated him and his clients many times over for the one that got away.

Can't-losers are not seeking gains so much as a feeling of infallibility or its continual confirmation. By compulsion they are the eternal optimists of this world.

Ehrenkranz Revisited

Louis Ehrenkranz, when he was a young broker in Brooklyn, seemed to collect can't-losers the way a bright light attracts moths. Louis was so affected by some of his experiences that he set them down in a letter to a friend. Here is a portion of Louis' letter:

"Murray Baron is very short and very fat. But what is most striking about Murray is his voice. It is very much like Jimmy Durante's voice in timbre, but louder. When Murray Baron rasps the time of day it has got to sound like one of the most important pieces of news since the atom bomb. But along with the raspy voice is an air of assurance that is merely a cover-up for the need thereof.

"The market break during the Cuban crisis did not treat Murray Baron's investments kindly. As I recall, he had 500 shares of MGM, 200 Brunswick, 300 Chock Full O' Nuts and 100 Gulton Industries. As the tension increased, these securities fell frighteningly. When I walked into my office Tuesday morning the phone was ringing. It was Murray: Jimmy Durante with hysteria. 'Lou,' he rasped, 'what are you doing to me?'

"I knew he had good cause for alarm but still I was

annoyed at his charging *me* with responsibility for his predicament; I explained that everybody was losing money.

'They are?'

'Of course.'

'How come? What's going on?'

'Mr. Baron, wake up! There's a possibility of war. With Russia.'

'So what?'

'A nuclear war!'

'That should make the market go down?'

'It could make all of us go down, Mr. Baron.'

'Real estate? My buildings? *Never!*'

'Mr. Baron, if there's going to be a war, forget it.'

'You really think so?'

'Yes.'

He hesitated, thoughtful, perhaps for the first time in his life. 'Louie, do you think there is going to be a war?'

'I don't know.'

'Don't hedge. I'm asking you a direct question. Will there be a war?'

'How the hell do I know, Mr. Baron?'

'What do I retain you for? I'll tell you. For information. You work for one of the biggest, right? They're the best, right? They spend millions on research, right? You want to be my broker? Find out if there's going to be a war or not!'

'Yes, Mr. Baron. Hang up, please, and I'll call the chairman of the board and ask him if there's going to be a war.' After waiting two or three minutes, trying to regain my mental balance, I called Murray Baron back. 'It's all right, Mr. Baron. No war.'

'You mean it, Louie? Listen. Buy 300 Gulton Industries, 200 White Consolidated, 100 Genesco, 300 Certainteed . . .'

"Not all the characters in Brooklyn were my clients. I didn't have the concession on eternal optimists, either. Take Mrs. Simpson, for example. One of the other brokers, Brian Flint, handled her, and beautifully. Mrs. Simpson didn't really care whether she made money or not—she merely wanted assurance. No matter how bad things really were Brian gave her the cheerful, optimistic side. I can still hear him droning reassuringly into the mouthpiece of his phone, 'Yes, it will be O.K., Mrs. Simpson, everything is going to be all right, I firmly believe that the market will go to an all-time high, you may be losing money now, Mrs. Simpson, but it's bound to change for the better, very soon. . . .'

"One day Brian was out when Mrs. Simpson phoned and I took the call.

'Mr. Flint's wire.'

'Is Mr. Flint in?'

'I'm sorry. Brian's out to lunch. Can I help you, Mrs. Simpson?'

'How's the market doing?'

'Badly. Down 13 points already.'

'What?'

'Utilities, motors, and steels are especially weak.'

'Isn't *anything* up?'

'No.'

'Won't they go up?'

'Not today, I'm afraid.'

'Tomorrow, then?'

'I don't think so.'

'Well, surely you're expecting a rally on Wednesday?'

'No. Frankly, Mrs. Simpson, the way things look I expect the market to keep going down.'

'I have one more question.'
'Yes?'
'What time will Brian be back from lunch?' "

Are there many like Mrs. Simpson and Murray Baron, who prefer not to face reality, can't-losers who want to know the truth only if it is reassuring and confirms their wisdom, who, as a consequence, spin their wheels with a loser, sinking in deeper and deeper before they can manage to make themselves let go?

Brokers estimate that 90 percent of the phone calls they receive are for the purpose of checking or affirming—in essence, to reinforce the caller's optimism.

11

The
Reluctant Dragons

In its next census of the U.S. shareholder population, the New York Stock Exchange might provide a bit of further enlightenment by estimating how many men and women now in the market shouldn't be in it and, what's more, don't want to be in it; also, what percentage of these reluctant dragons believe they are achieving a fair return on their invested capital.

Merely from observation and hearsay it would appear that to quite a few investors the market is a bad habit to be kicked; but like smokers who've been warned by a doctor or by their own sense of self-preservation, these shareholders keep deferring the day of decision. Not that many of them are boardroom bugs or trader types or stock addicts who must overdraw their bank accounts to satisfy a craving for securities; on the contrary. Most seem to be responsible, usually solvent citizens who have not visited a broker's office since the day their account was opened, if then, and who would be just as happy—or happier—curtailing their market activity. But for one reason or another that seems good and sufficient to them, they are participating in people's capitalism, however grudgingly, to the limit of either their emotional or financial resources.

Although for some of them shares of stock represent social credentials, another way of keeping up with the Joneses, in the main the reluctant dragons have little in common with the everyday tagalong or boom-time enthusiast of modest means who hopes to strike it rich in $2 offshore oils or Canadian mines. While it is patently impossible to guess who is in the market to make money and who to make conversation or to enhance status or to fill up the "golden" hours of retirement or even to accommodate somebody else, the investor's purpose is pertinent. Taste in stocks may be more or less expensive or more or less speculative, and social considerations may be more or less pressing, in individual cases, but the reluctant ones are distinguished by the *why* of their market activities rather than by the *what* or *how*.

The Accommodator

Miles, Sr., for example, might be characterized as an accommodator. Having profitably operated a family-owned business until age sixty-five, he then turned over his stock as well as his office to his oldest son, Miles, Jr., and retired with his wife to Clearwater, Florida, to live modestly but comfortably on the income from his savings, which amounted to about $300,000.

The accommodatee in this instance, Miles, Jr., was very ambitious and financially oriented. His first major action on succeeding to the presidency of the company was to make a public offering of stock—150,000 of his own newly acquired shares and 50,000 treasury shares— thus becoming an instant millionaire and also providing the company with funds for modernization of plant and equipment. At the time of the public offering, the son invited the father to purchase 2,000 shares at the issue price of $11, both as an investment and "because the name will look good on the record, like a vote of confidence from old management in new management."

Miles, Sr., was proud and happy to co-operate, of course, so much so that he suggested to his new friends and neighbors in Clearwater that they might want to purchase all the shares their brokers could obtain for them.

Junior proved to be a capable manager as well as a financial opportunist. Before long the company was showing earnings of almost $1 a share, every penny of which was plowed back into the business for expansion and the upgrading of personnel.

Since no dividends were paid, Miles, Sr., was doing without the interest he might have been receiving had the stock-purchase money remained in the savings bank. Worse yet, the increase in company earnings was inadequately reflected in the price of the stock now trading over-the-counter. The market seemed disinterested; trading was sparse. The trouble, as analyzed by Miles, Jr., was lack of liquidity; and the solution, he felt, was to put more shares in the hands of more people. Accordingly, he made another public offering, this time 100,000 shares of his own stock, through an underwriter who was careful to effect broad national distribution. An allocation of 1,000 shares was made available to Miles, Sr., and several thousand more shares to the old man's Florida friends. After the underwriting discount and legal fees, Miles, Jr., netted just about a million dollars for himself. Subsequently, the company was listed on the American Stock Exchange.

While he would never admit it to anyone, not even to his wife, privately Miles, Sr., was beginning to have mixed feelings about his stockholdings. Proud of his son's accomplishment and more than pleased to help make him rich, he was at the same time a bit uneasy about going into the market at his age, especially since the investment now represented over 10 percent of his total worth. What made him acutely conscious of his situation was not only the continuing lack of market support—the price had flattened out again within weeks after the stock was listed on the Amex—but also the fact that his retirement income was now reduced by about $1,800 a year.

After a while, under pressure from industry competition, Miles, Jr., was obliged to cut prices. Earnings declined. And the stock dropped. Junior was extremely put out, because he had been shopping the field for smaller companies with compatible product lines to acquire and to be paid for with shares. In his view, the market price of any stock was largely a matter of investor psychology and confidence. And the price-earnings ratio of his own stock was below the industry average, he reasoned, simply because there was no excitement about it. While the business did not lend itself to public relations ballyhoo, it should be possible to create an impression of excitement and to stir up some investor interest, he decided, by means of the market action itself. Since the daily trading volume averaged under 1,000 shares, even a small but steady influx of buyers might push the price back up to where it had been. Accordingly, Junior urged his father, along with other relatives, associates and friends to start accumulating additional stock, 100 shares at a time, every other day or so. If by their combined efforts they could double the skimpy volume and boost the price just a couple of points, Junior intimated, they might succeed in getting a bandwagon going that could eventually provide handsome capital gains opportunities for all of them, especially if he could top off the higher price levels by announcing completion of his acquisition negotiations.

Miles, Sr., was embarrassed because his Florida friends and neighbors were continually asking him what had happened to the company. When he protested to Miles, Jr., that he could not afford to keep a large sum of money invested in a declining stock that paid no dividends, his son suggested buying on margin. In that way, he argued, the old man would not have to divert any more of his savings but could use the value of his current stock holdings as buying power to purchase additional shares. But when Miles, Sr., opened a margin account and bought more shares of his son's company, he found that he was required to pay interest to his broker on the borrowed funds. He consoled himself with the thought that the situation was temporary; as soon as his active co-operation was no longer required he would sell all but a few hundred "token" shares and put the proceeds back into the bank.

To the disappointment of all the associates, relatives and friends of Miles, Jr., their market push failed to stimulate investor interest and soon the stock began to sag as a result of sharper industry competition and tighter profits. Not wishing to accept a big loss, Miles, Sr., held on to his shares. Then one day he received a margin call from his broker and to meet it he had to withdraw more of his savings from the bank.

Despite his son's proven ability and repeated assurances that sales would soon be up, that he would be diversifying into new higher-profit products, and that once the stock recovered sufficiently for him to consummate his acquisition plans, the company would declare a liberal dividend, the old man had begun to worry. While he did not for a moment doubt his son's word or his intentions, the fact remained that Miles, Sr., and a number of people he had to face almost every day were short money that they could ill afford to do without. Besides, he just did not have the temperament to take a roller-coaster ride with part of his retirement income.

It was five years ago when the old man decided definitely that he would withdraw from the stock market as soon as possible. He is still in it, however. He now owns over 4,000 shares of the same stock, worth less than he paid for it. He is out a substantial amount of the interest income on which he had counted. He has incurred additional brokerage commissions and interest charges in connection with his margin debt. He is concerned about his son's reputation. He no longer discusses his former business or his son's progress. And he has moved from Clearwater to St. Petersburg to avoid the questions of old friends and neighbors. When people he meets for the first time associate his name with that of the company he founded or ask him about the stock, he cuts the conversation short by saying that as an insider he cannot disclose any information, or refers them to a broker for facts and opinions. And he is still re-

solved that just as soon as he can dispose of his stock
—discreetly, that is, without bringing the price down
further—he will do so.

Executive on the Move

Another reluctant drag-on with a different reason for
being in the stock market and also a different reason
for being less than happy about it is Burt, who started
investing when he was an assistant divisional sales
manager in Southern California for one of the Big
Three auto manufacturers. Everybody he knew and
wanted to know talked about stocks. Burt was making
enough money, the market was going up, so why not?
But after he had been an investor for just about two
years, with a portfolio of four sound long-term growth
stocks worth about $20,000, Burt was suddenly trans-
ferred to Detroit as national sales promotion manager.
Unable to find a buyer for his house immediately and
eager to take possession of a new home in one of the
better Detroit suburbs so that his family could be
moved without delay, he decided to sell his stocks and
use the proceeds for a down payment. Unfortunately,
the market was just then experiencing one of its recurrent "corrections," and Burt had to take a loss of
about 5 percent on the sale of his stock.

After Burt's old house was finally disposed of, he
put $20,000 back into the market, which had fully re-
covered in the meantime. And for two years his annual
bonus money also went into stocks, long-term growth
issues with capital gain possibilities. Then Burt was
transferred again, this time as sales manager of a key
division headquartered in San Francisco. It was another

promotion for him but a costly one. Before he could get rid of his old house, he had to make a down payment on a new one. And once more he was compelled to sell his stock holdings and take a beating in the process, because the market was in a downtrend.

Four times within a period of ten years Burt sold securities in order to finance real estate transactions resulting from company-directed transfers. Although each time he came out ahead in terms of salary and bonuses, his net worth suffered, because he was selling stocks out of necessity rather than choice. He realized that he was being whipsawed, of course, and why. Were it not for the nonfinancial considerations of status —Burt's desire to hold his own in a group devoted mainly to cars, sports and stocks—he would have been out of the market and probably wealthier for it.

The Impresaria

A reluctant dragonette, under rather unique circumstances, was Maxine. Very astute but plain looking, a divorcee in her early forties, Maxine was impresaria and sole proprietor of an international artists bureau. Once a year she personally escorted a company of American concert artists or sometimes a theatrical attraction on tours that she had booked abroad. And once a year she personally escorted a company of continental artists on tours of major cities of the United States. Meticulous, cultured, well organized, as well as unattached, she had the ideal personality and background for an enterprise that involved both a great deal of travel and the ability to act as guide, interpreter and housekeeper for prima donnas and lesser exhibition-

ists. The money she earned—and it was quite a lot—
went into the bank against the day when she might no
longer be able or care to continue her strenuous business activities.

About ten years ago Maxine bought two stocks traded
over-the-counter, because she had heard some cocktail
talk about these particular issues that happened to be
booming at the time. Then she took to boning up on
the market at night in hotel rooms, considering the
effort more mature and potentially more rewarding
than reading novels or doping doublecrostics. Also, she
found, stocks gave her another bridge for communica-
tion with performers who tended to regard her as
necessary but not one of their own, not an artist but a
businesswoman.

While Maxine had the brains and character to become a successful investor, she lacked the time to concentrate on her investments and, frequently, the means
to reach her broker quickly enough. On tour, she was
caught up in scheduled performances, travel arrange-
ments, hotel accommodations, lost or mislaid baggage,
the press, sudden illnesses and artistic temperament—
though not necessarily in that order of importance.
During the brief interval between domestic and foreign
tours when she was in New York, Maxine was laying
her plans for the following season, corralling new artists
and making bookings. As a consequence, most of her
ideas for investment originated with other investors
encountered in the course of business or in her travels.

In 1962 Maxine learned the expensive way to stay out
of highly speculative, unlisted issues. After that she
invested strictly in leading companies with solid earnings, deliberately sacrificing some appreciation potential
for greater peace of mind. Still, she could not keep up

with her investments as closely as she felt she should.
The most informative press abroad as far as U.S. securities were concerned, the *International Herald* and the
Rome American, carried only a limited amount of financial news. It seemed frivolous to phone her broker
from Copenhagen or Munich with orders based on stale,
incomplete facts. While Maxine felt less remote on
her U.S. tours, she was still nervous, because few local
papers had anything like an adequate financial section,
not even stock tables in many cities, and the *Wall Street
Journal* was often unobtainable.

Each time the New York Stock Exchange index or
the Dow-Jones Industrial Average or one of her own
holdings slipped a notch—especially when she was
away from New York—Maxine feared another bad break
like the one in 1962. By the end of 1968 her portfolio
was substantial despite all handicaps and several serious losses. But Maxine was getting older and tired of
her strenuous, essentially lonely, life. Each season the
risk of losing any part of her hard-earned investment
frightened her more. Each time, before taking off, she
was tempted to pull out of the market entirely or to
convert her stocks into fixed-income securities. But
nothing that she could think of that might reduce the
risk could also offer the same opportunity to fatten the
cushion she felt she needed for retirement.

Even though her securities, above average in stability,
had performed reasonably well in all kinds of markets—
extremely well considering her disadvantages of time
and distance and mobility—Maxine had come to dread
the ritual of checking the latest prices in the newspapers. No matter how bullish the news, she could
not dispel the fear that next time she might find her
nest egg broken. And yet she never did bring herself

to the point of selling her holdings and putting the proceeds into bonds or savings. Then suddenly it was 1970: Her business was in recession and her portfolio was worth 25 percent less.

For various reasons of age or temperament or job insecurity or occupational mobility, there are many people who should not invest in common stocks although they can afford to. And there are many others who have reason to be investors but are in the wrong type of security or investment medium for their purpose. Consequently, they are unhappy about their participation and usually seem not to know what to do about it.

With about $300,000 saved up, Miles, Sr., had enough to insure a comfortable retirement had he invested in stocks to provide relatively high yield, around 5 percent, together with relatively low risk and moderate future prospects promised steady, non-cyclical long-term growth of at least 3 percent a year, so that the combined return from current yield plus basic earnings growth would come to over 8 percent a year. At almost any time he might have found a number of utilities to meet this standard as well as several attractive industrials. Or, by investing his money in a mutual fund offering a systematic withdrawal plan, he could have provided himself with 8 percent a year, part from dividends, the rest from principal. Either course would be predicated, however, on the proposition, most unlikely, that Miles, Sr., could have resisted the persuasions of his son and his own paternal pride.

Burt had no alternative but to talk stocks—and football and cars—if he wanted to be considered a regular guy and to hold his own in social give-and-take. But he might have gone about it in the same manner as some of his associates, undoubtedly, investing on a modest scale, no more than necessary to give substance to his contributions in brag sessions. As a matter of fact, with his income and record of progress in the company, he might have accepted the risk of an aggressive, though limited, portfolio aimed at maximum growth of capital over a relatively short time span. He could afford to assume high risk. What he could not afford was big commitment. As long as he kept himself reasonably liquid, in anticipation of future transfers, he had no cause to fear the stock market.

Like airline pilots and sales representatives and others whose work keeps them on the move, Maxine might have achieved better results with greater peace of mind had she been able to find someone to whom she could give limited discretion over her holdings, specifically the authority to make sell decisions under certain conditions in her absence. Undoubtedly she would be worth more today had she succumbed to earlier temptations and planned her retirement program around a more stable type of investment.

It is easy enough to say what others should have done with their money after the fact. It is more difficult and more enlightening, perhaps, to understand why people like Miles, Sr., and Burt and Maxine continue to do what they have been doing even though they are uncomfortable about it and are falling short of their objectives. One explanation is that return on investment, all-important as it should be, seems less important to some than another purpose, only indirectly related to the stock market and its moneymaking opportunities.

12

When I Want Advice,
I Ask a Rich Man

A young securities analyst who had been enjoying a hot hand in drugs, his industrial specialty, was standing around at a party, getting acquainted with his first cocktail of the evening, when from a nearby corner he caught the familiar drift of market talk. Approaching the group, all strangers, he heard the remark: "All you can expect from a stockbroker is a letter-perfect reading of the past record." At this point the young analyst, who took pride in his own professional competence, recognized the speaker as a TV personality and occasional character actor in plays and films.

Continuing to hold forth, the actor, who had a quick, sharp tongue along with a loud, round voice, maintained that older brokers still picked stocks by pulling names out of a bowler, while the new breed made their selections by punching random buttons on a computer; that anybody could make money in the market when it was going up and everybody lost money in the market when it went down, except the in crowd that had pulled the plug out; that research studies and reports were pretentious tout sheets; that he'd personally tried four different BIG brokers, partners or vice presidents of their respective firms, and not one had told him more than he could find out for himself in the pages of the *Times* and *The Wall Street Journal*. "Like I just collected 50 thou for some TV commercials. Man, I'd stick every penny in the market if I could find somebody who could tell me not why what happened yesterday happened, but what to do about it tomorrow."

"You're in luck," interjected their host, who had just come by. "We have a real Wall Street whiz kid here tonight."

As they were being introduced, the long-haired, middle-aged, Pierre Cardin-fashioned actor surveyed the young analyst from the smudged tips of his Thom McAn slip-ons to his No. 3 model Brooks Brothers suit and Tie City tie to his short, up-tight sideburns and crew-cut crown. "When *I* want advice," declared the would-be investor of $50,000, in a voice that projected to the kitchen, "I ask a *rich* man!" Whereupon he turned grandly on his heel and went off to refill his glass.

The put-down was notable only for the manner of delivery, not for the attitude expressed. It seems a perfectly logical assumption to a great many investors that those who know the most make the most money in the market, and that therefore those who make the most money must be those in the know. How could a $20,000-a-year researcher—or a $35,000-a-year broker, for that matter—possibly possess the kind of information that would make anyone rich? If he did, surely he would be the first to capitalize on his own knowledge and make himself independently wealthy. Instead of having to work for a salary or commissions in the service of others, the man who knew where profits were to be made would keep it all to himself. Or so the reasoning goes.

Every day of the week professional securities people hear levelers like these:

"You know so much, how come you're not rich instead of working nine to five?"

"I got this stock from a man that's *rich*."

"By the way, how are *you* making out in the market yourself?"

"Do you have many successful clients, I mean *really* rich?"

A widespread attitude, certainly; a logical one, perhaps; but superficial just the same. While brokers and securities analysts and investment advisers, most of them, would like to make as much money as they can, getting rich in the stock market requires more than ideas about stocks to buy and the time to buy them, indispensable as such information can be. The investor's character, habit patterns, life style, count for much more in the final analysis than the investment vehicle or the investment strategy. Indeed, some Wall Street pro's pros owe their success to a habit of *never* investing for themselves. By abstaining, they avoid any conflict between heart and head as well as possible confusion between client interests and self-interest. Stock market professionals who do invest for their own account— like doctors who prescribe medication for themselves—

experience a wide range of results from poor to spectacular.

A vice president of a venerable Wall Street investment banking house that maintains no branch offices, solicits no business from the public, and never advertises except for "tombstone" announcements of underwritings, private placements, mergers and acquisitions, functioning behind the scenes as market makers and underwriters of securities issues, tells of an experience while vacationing last winter in the British Virgin Islands. At the hotel bar he was engaged in conversation by a large, amiable young Oklahoman who talked about his family business—it supplied equipment to drillers of oil wells—until, having established his credentials, he inquired, "And what business you in, Suh?"

"Securities. Stocks and bonds."

"You don't say, now!" exclaimed the young man with warm interest. "We do quite a bit in the market, my dad and me. What firm you with, Suh?"

At the name of the investment banker's firm all interest faded from the young man's eyes. "Well, Suh," he said coolly, "personally, we always do business with the biggest fellows in town." After which he proceeded to empty his drink in silence.

The young man may be excused for assuming that anyone who identified himself with the securities business had to be a stockbroker, or for being unfamiliar with the name of a leading Wall Street investment banking house; but his reaction to what he took to be small and little known, and therefore insignificant, is symptomatic of a viewpoint that can be costly.

Innumerable investors make a point of giving their brokerage business to the most affluent—not necessarily the brightest or most experienced—securities man in their social circle. Countless others make a point of dealing only with the head man of a brokerage office, preferably a partner or vice president, even though these are likely to be administrative officers, up from the ranks, perhaps, but no longer as closely in tune with the market as the front-line boardroom brokers. Millions feel more confident about investing through a "big name" firm that may be better known for its advertising or plush offices than for its research or market executions. And there are some who take pride in an association with a broker or investment adviser who is making "an exception" for them, because he is "really too busy" to handle any more clients or because their account is "not large enough" for him to bother with, ordinarily.

The assurance of dealing with a busy, successful, well-to-do financial authority with a title to prove it, or with minimum dollar standards above their maximum reach, is essential to a certain type of investor who regards the rich man as having either special knowledge or the Midas touch. While it may appear uppity or naïve, the attitude probably denotes uncertainty or fear. The man or woman who will take financial advice only from someone who is known to be wealthy wants to believe that he or she thus obtains the secret formula or, at the very least, immunity from criticism should the decision turn out to be a mistake.

If you seek the advice of a rich man and it proves to be wrong, it's *his* mistake, if you like, not yours. Since you sought the best advice obtainable and you followed that advice to the letter, you can't be criticized one little bit. And rich men can afford to be fallible. On the other hand, had you listened to a hard-working broker or investment adviser whose net worth is no greater than your own, you might be taking a tall chance. If the advice turned out to be wrong, you'd have no one to blame but yourself.

Not infrequently, the investor who places face above all pays a stiff premium—willingly or otherwise—for the preservation of his dignity.

Ironically, the face-saver type is as common on Wall Street as on Main Street. Recently a vice president of a leading advertising agency, who had succeeded in developing an effective marketing strategy and an attractive public image for a national retail brokerage organization, decided to open an agency of his own that would specialize in financial advertising and public relations. Sounding out prospective clients, he lunched with top executives of several large Wall Street firms. He kept receiving polite brush-offs until one of the financial executives told him frankly: "You'd be making a mistake if you came downtown and opened your own shop. I happen to respect what you've accomplished but we're just discovering advertising down here, so we don't know enough about it yet to have confidence in our own judgment. We prefer to place our business with either of the two old-established financial agencies downtown or with one of the major, established consumer agencies, like yours, uptown, because we know that if things turn sour we can point out that we were advised by one of the recognized authorities. That takes the monkey off our back. But if we entrust our name to somebody without a reputation, we're vulnerable. Even if we get fine results, our judgment is suspect for gambling. And if the results we get are questionable, we'll be criticized for it, believe me. It's not just advertising, either.

If you were a smart young lawyer and thinking about starting your own law firm downtown, I'd tell you the same thing. Come to work for us or join a well-established firm down here and maybe we'll listen to you. But if you were to try it on your own without the kind of reputation we could fall back on to protect ourselves against criticism, I'd have to wish you well and suggest you offer your services to one of our competitors."

In other words, when I want advice, I ask the man who is best qualified as a potential scapegoat!

13

The

Hyperactivists

The president of a listed company was comparing himself with his old friend and executive vice president, in terms of market approach. "Me," said the president, "I just buy, I never sell. I buy quality and sit back and let inflation boost the value of my investment. Maybe I'm just lucky but I've made lots of money in the market doing it my way. Now look at Stan," the president went on. "He's a millionaire, sure, but he could be a two-millionaire if he'd just sit with his stock a while. But no, he's in and out, swinging around, trying to come in on the lows and get out on the highs, every single time. And sometimes I suspect he doesn't even care about *that*, he just likes to be giving orders to his broker. I'll give you an example. We both bought our first shares of Polaroid about the same time, years ago. By now I must own a couple thousand shares, with an adjusted base price around $2 or so. But Stan, he's still about where he was—taking 10 or 15 point profits or losses on 100 or 200 shares at a time. I can't understand why he bothers to buy the stock if he doesn't intend to keep it. He certainly isn't making more money his way."

Dozens of seasoned Wall Streeters were asked if they knew—or knew of—an active trader who had outperformed the market over a full cycle, that is, through boom, decline and back around again. Not one answered in the affirmative. If there are any consistently successful short-term traders in the market they are not conspicuous. The unsuccessful ones, however, are legion and legend.

Here are two cases, more or less representative.

A partner in a brokerage firm tells about a client of his, worth $40 million, who used eleven different brokers to feed him trading ideas and to execute his orders. He bought big, very big, according to the broker, "trying to win enough to crow about or lose enough to really hurt so he could feel sorry for himself." Once he bought a stock, it was this swinger's custom to phone the broker three times in the morning and three times in the afternoon to check out the prices. As soon as a stock had moved up two or three points, the order was, "Sell!" With stocks that moved *down* the trader was inclined to be more indulgent. He liked to take profits, not losses, so he tended to let his losers accumulate. Since his profit margins were narrow and his loss margins wide, he lost a great deal of money and, consequently, could feel sorry for himself much of the time. But the sorriest aspect of his trading

activities was that he spent so many hours of his working day on the phone with brokers that he lost touch
with his main business. Eventually he had to retire so
that he could trade stocks without being distracted by
profitable concerns.

A wealthy lady who craved winning as well as
action gave her broker a large sum of money and
with it full discretion to follow a trading list put
out by a popular technician. Thus, the broker had
full authority to buy or to sell—up to the limit of
the money he had been given—without consulting
his client. The idea was to permit him to act without
delay on any opportunity recommended by the technician. The broker did his best to help his client
justify her proud boast that she was "a natural winner."
Over the better part of a year, during a rising market,
the lady gained about 25 percent on her money and
felt rather pleased with herself. When political and
economic uncertainties caused the stock market first
to wobble and then to slump, the technician's trading
list lost its magic. It worked for upswings exclusively,
it seemed. But nobody knew that as yet, not even
the technician. The broker kept buying and selling
off the trading list, as he was expected to do. And
the hyperactive lady wound up a loser by close to
20 percent.

From all the evidence and testimony of brokers,
if any approach to the market can be called self-
defeating it is that of the short-term trader. Even
when there is a quick gain of a few points, there
may be no profit. After paying brokerage commissions
in and out, a transfer tax, high interest rates on margin
debt, and income tax on a short-term capital gain,
the hyperactivist is lucky to break even.

Another obstacle: the swinger is apt to be buying at or near the upper limit of a stock's advance, then selling after the reaction sets in.

By contrast with the long-term investor who can ignore day-to-day fluctuations and concentrate on the potential value of his holdings, the short-term trader is often at the mercy of market trends. He takes big risks going in when prices are high and his stocks offer relatively little upside potential. And in a declining market he not only takes bigger risks, he also misses out on the best opportunities; for a downdraft can pull in even exceptional values which, with patience, could produce exceptional profits.

Whether he likes it or not, the hyperactivist must get used to large losses and puny profits, simply because bad situations tend to deteriorate faster than good ones develop.

Buying smart is not nearly as much trouble as selling smart. While there is never any compulsion to buy in a hurry, there may be very compelling reasons to sell promptly. Also, while there are usually many good buys in the market, there is rarely a "good" stock to sell. So the in-and-outer must rely on extra-sensory perception or else on a formula—so many dollars or so much percentage up or down. But trading formulas have seldom had any more success over the long term than E.S.P.

Where the investor is in a position to put away good stocks, checking them periodically, the trader must be as close as a shadow to the movements of his stocks. Close attention demands time and concentration. In a busy market some traders tend to become hypnotized by the moving symbols on the boardroom tapes, with the result that they can't tear themselves away from the action long enough to attend to their business or profession. Not a few end up as boardroom bums.

And yet frequent trading is the one and only way for tens of thousands of adults, many of them intelligent, responsible, otherwise successful people.

Except perhaps in a terminal situation like Hong Kong (where the long-term prospect is a return of the leased territories to China), the short-term trader must be motivated by other than financial factors. First of all, he is not buying value or estimated worth or potential but a ride on the price swings that characterize the law of supply and demand in action; so he is not an investor or even a speculator but a gambler. Next, the swinger is restless and impatient; he dotes on activity and variety. He likes to make decisions and snap off orders. The hustle-bustle of the boardroom or the business of dialing his broker at regular intervals during the day and getting a busy signal (most of the time) helps the hyperactivist feel that he's at the center of where it's all happening. In a certain sense he may be called a romancer, as opposed to a marrier. He intends to have his fun while remaining relatively free and uncommitted. Or he's willing to settle for smaller slices of lots of pies rather then restrict his scope.

The hyperactivist's rationale, when he bothers to offer one, for selling on a few points gain is that "you can't go broke taking a profit." Yet that is just what many short-term traders do.

The only ones sure of succeeding over the long run are the market masochists who are out to lose.

Most swingers, undoubtedly, are eager to win, to impress somebody, to show how smart they are, and to beat the system by buying in the valleys and selling on the mountains. And the winner truly believes that he's earned his profits, because he hasn't just lasted out the race like the tortoise-investor or had it happen to him like Sleeping Beauty; he's *made* it happen, just as he meant to.

The question occurs: If roulette were as respectable as the stock market and could be played over the phone through most of the business day, who would the hyperactivist be phoning more frequently, his broker or his croupier?

A composite profile of the swinger drawn from the perceptions of brokers and psychologists looks like this:

1. He likes to think of himself as a winner.
2. He gets a thrill out of taking financial risks.
3. He regards the market as a personal challenge, and trading as a test of his own acumen and nerve.
4. He likes an "aggressive" broker who will give him ideas for big profits in the shortest possible time.
5. His goals are point-blank range, of course, and he likes change for the sake of change, which gives him a sense of participating in the market news.
6. He tends to make his decisions quickly and then, often, to rationalize on the basis of information or chart readings.
7. He positively enjoys telling his broker not only what to do but also when to do it and how.
8. Unlike the professional trader or specialist on the floor, who tends to be unemotional about his business and rarely takes his trades, good or bad, home with him, the swinger would quit the market forever if he couldn't talk about his Syntex at 250 or

his IBM at 396, even if he *wasn't* there when it happened. If he didn't believe—or couldn't make others believe—that he was going to make waves on Wall Street, the hyperactivist would find another big-risk, big-payout challenge to test himself against.

While the hyperactivist pays in dollars and talks in eighths and quarters of a point, his real pursuit is action, and this is what he usually settles for.

According to our friendly neighborhood psychiatrist again, "The more active, the more egocentric, because he's looking for gratification of his desires and hopes not a few years from now and not six months from now but right now, immediately! His market inclinations follow the general psychic pattern of active versus passive tendencies. He is basically a passive person who needs to prove otherwise."

Psyche and personality aside, the fundamental mistake of the short-term trader, in the metaphorical view of one city-bred broker, is that "he cuts his roses when they're just beginning to bud, and lets his weeds just grow and grow."

14

The
Hedgers

The most talked-about hedger on Wall Street is a gentleman who works there, as it happens, as senior vice president of a trust company. In 1935 he inherited $12 million. In 1969 it was his proud boast that "I still have that $12 million." Incredible as it may seem to a less conservative type, this Wall Street professional knowingly and deliberately set out to keep his principal intact, and succeeded. Even so, it may be hard to see how anyone, however knowing and deliberate, could contrive to invest in securities and refrain from seeking *some* appreciation through at least the last twenty of those thirty-five years.

Hedgers are a breed apart. Brokers who have dealt in arbitrage, convertible bonds, and puts and calls, and sold against the box for years don't pretend to understand the personalities of their hedging clients. Cautious, conservative, afraid, are the usual descriptives, accompanied by a look or gesture of what-can-you-do?

Among wealthy, sophisticated investors, those who hedge presumably don't want or need more as much as they want or need to preserve what they already have. Those not so well endowed use hedging devices to speculate at reduced risk or for mainly psychological benefits.

A few examples.

Your alma mater receives an unexpected gift of 100,000 shares of ZYX. At the time, the market as a whole is shaky, though ZYX is selling at its historic high, which may suggest a reason for the suddenness of the tax-deductible gift. As a trustee, you naturally wish to preserve for Alma Mater the full value of the 100,000 shares, now quoted at 39½–¾. But you fear that if you just stick the stock away in Alma Mater's portfolio, it may go down along with the rest of the market. What can you do to insure against serious loss? Your first thought, probably, is a private placement. If you could get an institution—or even ZYX Company itself—to take the shares off your hands *right now*, you would be willing to concede 2½ points, or $250,000. After your broker has checked out several likely prospects, with negative results, you conclude that the institutional buyers are just as apprehensive as you are about a sharp drop in ZYX. Now you may start to consider hedging devices: either to sell against the box or else to issue security options. If you sell short against the 100,000 shares in Alma Mater's strongbox, and should ZYX subsequently fall out of bed, as you fear, your profit on the short sale offsets your loss in the market value of the stock; and should ZYX advance, counter to expectations, your loss on the short sale is exactly offset by the profit in the stock retained. Either way you have protected the value of the gift to Alma Mater. Let's say, however, that you and your fellow trustees decide that your 100,000-share block of ZYX is too large to sell short in this market. You might start kicking around the idea of issuing options. You would be in pretty good company, since about 30 percent of the puts and calls are issued by institutions, the rest by individuals with substantial holdings. Now if you sell calls on ZYX, and should ZYX subsequently go up enough for the options to be exercised, you will receive the current market price of 39½, approximately, plus a premium for issuing the options; and should ZYX go down subsequently, the options will not be exercised and the premiums you receive should offset, at least in part, the price erosion of the stock. In view of the fact that less than half of all issued stock options are ever exercised, chances are pretty good that Alma Mater would keep its ZYX and pick up a little extra cash on the premiums—assuming, of course, that you could sell enough options on ZYX to cover your 100,000 shares.

Now you are no longer acting as a trustee of Alma Mater; you're concerned with your own personal portfolio. Somewhere you've heard about ZYX and what you heard prompted you to ask for an opinion from your broker, who sent you a recent study by a securities analyst. From all you've heard and read up to this point you're inclined to believe that the stock has an excellent chance of advancing from 39½, its present price, to 60 or even higher, in six months to a year.

The trouble is, the market is in an uncertain phase and ZYX is the kind of volatile stock that could go down 10 points as fast as it could go up 20. Would you buy it? Even if you can afford to lose $1,000 financially, can you afford to lose it emotionally? Can you endure the cold sweats of worrying? Or should you hedge? For $500 or so you can buy a call on 100 shares of ZYX. Should ZYX go up to, say, 48 during the period of your option, you could exercise your call, assured of a small profit if you cared to sell immediately, or of a small cushion against future price decline if you wanted to hold the stock. Should ZYX fail to go up enough to entice you, you would be out $500, the cost of the option.

If your luck were average, you would have about four chances in ten of exercising your option. Or put another way, you would have to pay 10 premiums of 10–20 percent each in order to exercise your options four times; and you would have to anticipate a rise of at least 40 percent, each time, just to break even. At such odds, who would buy puts and calls? Conservative investors seeking insurance against deterioration of a market position sometimes resort to puts. And speculators seeking bigger profits from comparatively modest commitments of cash or courage often favor calls.

Frank, a professional hedger—he manages a hedge fund—uses puts and calls to play around with highly speculative stocks that he wouldn't dream of marrying. Take a trading favorite like Carolina Fried Chitlins, for example. Chitlins is a stock that Frank would not care to buy, because he feels that at $80 and 35 times earnings the downside risk equals the upside potential and a one-to-one-shot is not his idea of a smart speculation. On the other hand, if he has a hunch that Chitlins may be good for a brief fling, Frank can buy a six-month call for approximately $1,200. By so doing, says Frank, "I have taken odds that were once 50 points up, 50 points down, and limited my downside risk as a call holder of Chitlins to 12 points. Now, whether Chitlins goes up 6, down 6, or down 60, my downside risk is just 12 points. By buying a call instead of the stock, I've converted my risk-reward ratio from something as low as one-to-one, which doesn't interest me at all, to a ratio of approximately four-to-one, should it work out."

Before *you* used any hedging device, of course, you would check on your tax situation, including the possible consequences of short-term gains from options and short sales. But you'd be surprised how many inveterate hedgers don't bother. And therein lies a clue to their personality: incautiously cautious; afraid but rash.

Here's how one intelligent man, hooked on hedging by way of security options, explains his approach: "When I shell out for a premium on a call, I know exactly how much I can lose right off the bat. So I say to myself, okay I've blown the $600 or whatever the premium is, it's lost, gone forever. So I don't have to worry about it anymore. Hell, I can afford to blow $600 and I shouldn't have to stew about it. But it's all relative, you see. If I bought the stock outright, it would cost me $5,000 and I'd be sweating out the closing prices every afternoon to see if I was losing and how much. Maybe I'm kidding myself, because I've shelled out a hell of a lot of dough on premiums, but at least it's limited to what I know I can sleep with every time."

Instead of using options to cut downside risk, the penny-ante *gamblers* hope to stretch their upside potential. For the price of a call they buy themselves the illusion of larger stakes. But even when they are able to pick up their options, subsequent gains may not offset their cumulative premium costs.

The penny-ante *safety-firsters,* on the other hand, may have all kinds of money but are afraid to commit themselves, afraid to make a big mistake. They are looking for prior confirmation, a sure thing, or else an out. On a call, they are tranquilized by the thought that they don't actually have to buy the stock until it has gone up enough to show a small profit. At the race track, the same types would bet $2 across the board on the odds-on favorite or, perhaps, $2 on three horses in the same race, each to win. They want winners more than they want winnings.

15

The
Compleat Investor

After inspecting a dozen more or less self-imposed
roadblocks, it might appear as if we can't get there
from here; that by the process of elimination we have
left ourselves no way to advance. Have we been dem-
onstrating the proposition that investment success
is unachievable? Not deliberately. Are we trying to
suggest that while there may be plenty of losing habits,
negative patterns, there are no positive combinations
of character traits that lead to winning performance?
In other words, if you fail, is it your own fault?
and if you succeed, is it in spite of yourself? Or
does it come down to emotional hygiene: strip away
the bad habits once they are recognized for what
they are, and let yourself go? Nothing at all like
that.

Performance in the market—let's come right out and say it—seems more a matter of art than science, a view that may disquiet those who feel more comfortable with "absolute" verities than with relative values. But what are financial objectives if not dreams and hopes expressed as numbers? The artist creates his own heaven or hell with any media he can command, visual, verbal, kinetic, philosophical, plastic or numerical. Why not? For the investor as well as for the studio artist, conception and execution are governed every step of the way by imagination, temperament and judgment.

By definition, if you like, science teaches us to know, and art to do. Science is knowledge systematized, formalized. While art is knowledge made efficient by the application of individual skill.

If the investor, as practitioner, is an artist, the broker, as gatherer and arranger of facts, is a scientist—a distinction that may help account for many of the misunderstandings that arise between customer and customer's man. It may also help explain why some excellent economists, brokers and securities analysts perform poorly as investors. In the market, where science leaves off, art begins.

Central and basic to both, however, is knowledge, information, without which there is nothing for the broker to formalize, nothing for the investor to try his skills on. The investor without facts is like any artist without an idea: no reason to bother. In the beginning, at least, there must be an idea, a fact, or an appraisal, usually expressed in numbers. For some, the numbers may inspire beautiful dreams; for others, nightmares; for most, nothing at all. That is why, given one and the same set of facts, a few investors will buy, fewer still will sell short, the large majority will remain doubtful or indifferent. However objectively the facts may have been arrived at, their reception will be largely subjective, reflecting the receiver, his reflexes, preconceptions, and powers of evaluation, in short, his life style.

Of course, there can be more or less to an investment idea than a set of numbers. People, for instance; an appraisal of management. But in the beginning as in the end the sum of the broker's science may be represented by some such disciplined numerical arrangement as this: downside risk 10 percent, upside potential 40 percent.

Good brokers are generally numbers people. They express themselves naturally and fluently in terms of mathematical relationships. But while numbers may inspire the investor to try his skills, from the moment he starts to consider an order to buy or sell or hold, what may have been a simple and reasonable mathematical statement—like 10 percent downside risk, 40 percent upside potential, over a term of twelve to eighteen months—becomes a complex, inconsistent element in an essentially emotional process compounded of hope mixed with fear, common sense struggling against avarice, and logic butting up against premonition. What's more, as human beings, the broker-scientist and the investor-artist are both fallible. The risk-reward appraisal may turn out to be a miscalculation in the light of subsequent developments within the company or the industry. Or the time element may be affected by unpredictable events, national or international. In any case, after the broker has done his fallible or brilliant best in assembling the facts, it is up to the fallible investor to carry out his investment objectives in the face of ever-changing conditions whose duration and severity may be known to no one. In addition, he must cope with himself, with all his habits, good and bad, with all his qualities of mind and heart, both strong and weak. Where the broker's business involves disciplined procedures, the shareholder's *modus operandi* is often a matter of personality.

It is perhaps in the hope of turning risky, tricky art into something more businesslike that many investors make use of such scientific trappings as charts, graphs, moving averages, and other technical paraphernalia, and why many others hedge when there may be little to gain by it.

One persistent drawback with numbers as a source of investment inspiration is that those representing the past come too late to yield a profit, and those reflecting the future are mere conjectures, expectations, the dreamer's dream fulfilled.

Still, who can argue against the wisdom of being well informed, in possession of the known facts as well as the educated projections from those facts, the estimates? If facts and estimates were not so important, why would dozens of millions of dollars be lavished on securities research and analysis by the major brokerage firms? Reviews, market letters, weekly outlooks, monthly roundups, quarterly surveys, annual studies, comprehensive portfolio analyses, computerized stock opinions—the combined output of the brokers must add up to billions of numbers and words each and every market day; all for the purpose of informing the investor or keeping him informed.

And yet for all the brains and time and money and paper expended, some of the information offered is useful and timely, and some is not so useful; or it is premature, or just a trifle stale. No analyst, broker or investment adviser issues a guarantee with his information, only hope and a piece of his reputation. The professionals know that their advice, though printed in two colors under the house logotype, is written in shifting sands. The least wind of fortune—a government contract awarded or canceled, an industry-wide strike settled or called, the drift of war clouds abroad—can scramble the carefully composed words and numbers into a mocking monument to the composer. In short, while it may be very wise to keep informed and to take advantage of available research facilities, there is more to market wisdom than being well informed.

Timing is a critical factor. Sophisticated investors like to point out that the right security at the right price is not right enough. It may sit there indefinitely at the same price level. Or it may go down before it goes up. The right time, *when* to buy, *when* to sell, they insist, is the clincher. Fine and dandy, except that nobody can confidently predict the future. The past? Easy. The past can be described accurately and fully, it can be abstracted onto charts and graphs and tables and IBM printouts. But the future? *Projections:* thoughtful, hopeful, worried, desperate, or electronically automated extensions of the known into the unknown and unknowable.

Does the better informed investor make more money in the stock market? Not always. An excess profits tax on the gains of all the uninformed successes would put a substantial dent in the national debt. Obviously, information can help an investor reach a decision—the more timely the information and the keener the investor's judgment, the happier the decision might turn out—up to a point. No doubt, useful information can help astute investors make bigger profits or take smaller losses by shading the odds a bit in their favor. But there is much more to *useful* information than a reliable, timely idea.

As an extreme example, let's suppose that by some nightmarish coincidence each of the 30,000,000 shareholders in the United States received exactly the same buy or sell recommendation. And then let's assume that a mere 1 percent, or 300,000, decided to act upon the information. What would happen? Is there a listed or unlisted stock that could withstand the pressure, that would not be driven through the roof or the cellar? Unimaginable? All right, let's suppose only 1,500 of the 7,500 major institutions—banks, insurance companies, foundations and mutual funds— assisted by their ever-watchful copycat computers spotted the same significant trend in a stock, and that just 150 sought to buy, say, an average of 10,000 shares each. What would happen to the price even if the stock was as widely held as Telephone?

Actually, today hundreds of thousands of investors— clients of any one of the larger brokerage houses—may be exposed to exactly the same fact, opinion or news flash. And the information is mostly reliable; it has to be, in a highly competitive industry. Researchers who are right get raises and titles; those who are not don't last very long. The advice is the best that serious money can buy, for there is probably not a securities analyst or an investment house that strives for less than 100 percent rightness. Fortunately—and curiously—however, out of one hundred investors receiving identical buy recommendations from the very same broker, about ninety will react negatively, doubt-

fully, or not at all, and ten may respond affirmatively.
And among these ten there will be a wide dispersion
pattern; that is, some will act sooner than others,
the amounts of money involved will vary, and some
will sell within the year while others will hold indefinitely.

If usually timely, reliable information is not enough
for ninety out of one hundred investors, there must
be other factors at work. The financial situation at
the moment. Mental state, optimistic or pessimistic.
Who made the recommendation. What other people
say about it. Judgment in evaluating the information.
And pre-conditioning: One man will not buy the stocks
of retailers, department stores or chains, all of which
seem insubstantial to him; one woman will not buy
the stock of equipment or machinery companies (gross,
unesthetic, she couldn't take pride in ownership); "re-
spectability" of portfolio is a factor for one, who selects
a company for investment as he might a future son-in-
law, considering name, reputation, and antecedents
as well as prospects; for another, familiarity breeds
contempt, and he will not buy into companies or
industries with which he has had any association.

Whatever the source, no matter how thoroughly
researched or how cogently presented, any recommendation goes through a series of organic filters—brain,
heart and bankbook—before being fed into the creative
crucible of the prospective investor. Will the excitement
of a rising, high-volume market prove to be a positive
stimulus? Or will the fast pace of the market generate
fear and distrust? Does an uptrend suggest further
opportunities or, on the contrary, that the train has
been missed? Is the comparative quiet of a calm,
steady market deadly dull? Or is it reassuring?

What turns on the swinging risk taker turns off the safety-of-principal seeker. What encourages the latter bores the former.

It is not the investment that succeeds or fails, it's the investor.

What divides the winners from the losers? In many, many cases the difference can be traced to objectivity or the lack of it. Even professional money managers sometimes find it tough to maintain perspective, to keep cool in a crisis, to hold an aim and stay on top of holdings, regardless of the stakes or the pressure. But they try, because they know that without detachment they are amateurs.

Here is a case record of an amateur whose detachment was *almost* professional.

Arnie was a bright young C.P.A., a bachelor. As a pastime when he had nothing else to do in the evening, he liked to study financial statements and read up thoroughly on companies offering one or more of the following seven attractions:

1. A technological breakthrough
2. A new proprietary process
3. A change in management or policies that could turn a declining company around
4. An operational change that could reduce inventories or costs
5. A product innovation
6. Participation in an emerging growth industry
7. Merger or acquisition possibilities

When Arnie found a soundly financed company with one of these appealing attributes, he put it down in a ledger as a "pick" and he followed the stock as assiduously as if he owned it.

On paper Arnie was phenomenal. Over a period of two years, six of his seven picks appreciated in price. For a total hypothetical commitment of $32,000, Arnie's net "profit" amounted to $69,000, a return of over two for one.

Then Arnie got married and he had no lonely hours to fill for a while. When the novelty of marriage wore off, however, he resumed his study of financial data and again began to put down his picks in his ledger and to follow them closely.

When Arnie's wife discovered what he was doing for hours at a time by himself, she was pleased, especially after she saw how well he was doing at it in his ledger. She encouraged him, pointing out that one day they would need a second bedroom; that meanwhile the winters were cold and an otter coat would be very warm; that their apartment might be sweltering in summer but a small car would transport them to the cool breezes of the Jersey shore on weekends.

Arnie tried to make it clear that while his paper investments cost nothing but time, 100 shares of a $50 stock, if actually purchased, cost exactly $5,000 plus brokerage commission; and that they had in their savings bank at the moment precisely $1,352.19. Still his wife persisted until Arnie relented and compromised. He bought an active, promising $11 stock that met none of his seven criteria and which he was lucky enough to get out of at 9⅞. Arnie's wife was disappointed but not disheartened. Far from it. So Arnie, to appease her, bought 100 shares each of two

$5 stocks mentioned by one of his clients. His reason for buying *two?* To spread the risk. One of the $5 stocks promptly went up to eight. Arnie took the profit, tempted to call it quits for good while he was a bit ahead. But his wife was now more convinced than ever that Arnie could make them rich. So Arnie went on picking, limited by his bank balance to low-priced issues, intimidated by his wife's high expectations, resolved to make one quick, grand killing and then declare both his financial and marital independence by retiring from the market until such time as he was in a position to stick to his seven-cardinal-criteria approach. As it turned out, he continued to dribble away his savings on compromises and, in the process, his wife's high hopes and her respect for him.

The skillful amateur, having turned pro without the necessary resources, emotional or capital, could not stick to his investment standards under pressure. It is not only the amateur, however, who pays for the privilege of weighing and counting himself in the stock market.

Alan is the floor partner half of a two-partner "special situations" firm that you will never see advertised or cited by financial writers. Originally, Alan's job was to execute orders phoned down to the floor by his "upstairs" partner, Ray. Since their firm handled a limited number of very large accounts, Alan was not overworked by orders from clients. Having some time and being young, restless and aggressive, Alan had taken to acting as a "$2 broker" for an old-line investment banking firm, in its arbitrage operations, whenever there was more business than could be handled through its own floor partners. An exceptionally capable trader with a remarkable feel for the market, Alan was soon participating in virtually all the larger firms's arbitrage orders on the floor. Alan loved working with the super pros of Wall Street, the backstage handicappers who doped out the odds on projected mergers and acquisitions—even to the point of calculating which judge would be presiding if and when the Justice Department tried to block the deal. Based on the "handicaps," Alan might be buying a big block of stock while another floor broker representing the same investment banking firm might simultaneously be selling the convertible bonds. Or Alan might be selling short 15,000 shares on one side of the deal while at the same time another floor broker was buying 50,000 shares, in a carefully handicapped hedge. Or Alan might be buying rights to subscribe to a stock, knowing that another floor broker was already selling the securities that would eventually be obtained through the rights.

This type of activity was much more exciting for Alan than handling the usual run of client orders for a few hundred or a few thousand shares. He was a "natural" trader—or so everybody told him. Soon Alan began to ask himself why he wasn't engaged in these fascinating, lucrative trades for his own account instead of for just a modest piece of the brokerage.

Talking it over with his partner, Alan proposed that he become a registered trader, which would allow him to trade on the floor in stock in which he or his firm had a financial interest. Ray reluctantly agreed, and the two partners put up an additional $250,000 to satisfy the capital requirements of the New York Stock Exchange.

Happy and confident, Alan began doing for himself what he had been doing so successfully for others. He had never before worked so hard or enjoyed himself as much. In his first month as a registered trader Alan netted a $12,000 profit for his firm's account. An auspicious start. In the second month, though Alan made even more trades, the firm netted only $1,600 in its own account. In the third month Alan slowed down and the results were inconsequential. When at the end of the fourth month the firm's trading account showed a loss, the two partners held a conference.

Said Alan: "Ray, you've been great these past four months, you haven't criticized me once. But I've been criticizing myself, believe me. *I just can't do it.* There's something wrong with me. I've got to stop trading and go back to just executing orders. It seemed so easy, I was getting all those compliments when I was trading with someone else's money. But it's different with our money. Ray, honest, I'm not playing it cool anymore, I'm freezing up. I look at both sides carefully. Too damn carefully. I think about the stakes and ask myself how sure I am that I'm right. Then I have to push myself to take a position. Even if I'm right, I'm always just a little late. The trouble is—and I hate to admit it—I've lost my objectivity. Either that or I've lost my guts."

Alan went back to executing client's orders phoned down to the floor by Ray; and for fun he acted as a $2 broker, handling large arbitrage orders for others. When he was sorely tempted to trade for his own account again, he made bets on football or baseball games instead.

Another case record—call this one "Husbands and Lovers," with names and numbers doctored, of course—may help to document the critical importance of objectivity in the utilization of information, even the most factual and trustworthy.

Laura was emotionally dependent on her husband, and Walt was totally devoted to his business. That's the way it had been for as long as they had known each other. The early years of their marriage had been a grim financial struggle. Walt owned a tiny diner not far from Sportsman's Park, home of the old St. Louis Browns. To help out—and also to be near Walt—Laura worked over the grill while her husband served the customers. The constant heat from the grill made her skin greasy and turned her fine hair into strands of rope. Many a blistering summer afternoon, before the Browns moved and the ballpark was torn down, Laura, a college graduate, peddled hot dogs on the street to the fans. She hated what she looked like, but she did it for Walt.

As Laura saw him, Walt was an elemental force, tough, tireless, intelligent, and indomitable. His toughness made her feel protected. His intelligence and indomitability gave her confidence in the future. She believed that one day Walt would have everything he wanted, and so would she, because he was generous in his way. She knew what she wanted, too. When Walt had reached his goal, she wanted to move to New York or San Francisco where, she felt, they could get more out of their lives. Then they would travel, to Paris, Rome, Vienna, Madrid, London, in that order. In short, they would elevate and broaden themselves. And her clear vision of the future sustained her through the hot hours over the grill and under a midday sun, also through three difficult pregnancies. The children, fortunately, more or less raised themselves while Laura made herself available to Walt.

Their first big break from drudgery came out of Walt's idea to push doughnuts as high-profit, no-labor items. This one simple, obvious idea gave rise eventually to the national chain of Walt's Donut and Coffee Shops, an enterprise that was a dozen years in the building. While Laura ran the old diner, the original Walt's, her husband opened a second place. Once this was firmly established, Walt opened a third. Laura almost never saw him standing up or dressed anymore. It was only in bed that they came together, one of them asleep, the other exhausted.

When Walt's Donut and Coffee Shops numbered thirty-three, in seven states, he came to the conclusion that he could make more profit more consistently by assuring his source of supply. It was his second simple, obvious, but sound idea. Accordingly, he bought a majority interest in a doughnut bakery and not long after that began to accumulate stock in a flour mill that supplied the bakery. Pretty soon he had a controlling interest in the flour mill and was learning all about hedging in the commodities markets.

While Laura was exceedingly proud of Walt's growth, both in capacity and in achievement, she was frustrated by his unrelieved absorption in making money. Her one hope was that someday soon Walt would have made all the money he could possibly use, and would then stop working long enough to spend some in a meaningful manner.

About the time their oldest daughter was entering college, Laura helped Walt celebrate his first million. Walt commemorated the occasion by setting up a

$100,000 trust fund for Laura and for each of their three girls. Early the next morning he was hard at work on his second million.

Laura was no longer sweating it out behind the counter, of course. But idleness did not suit her, either. While she now had ample opportunity to do "meaningful" things, she did not care to do anything alone. She bought clothes, she dieted, she lavished care on her skin and hair, hoping that Walt would notice and say something to her; but he didn't. Since Walt was involved more and more in the stock market and matters of business finance, Laura enrolled in a correspondence course on investment theory and practice given by the New York Institute of Finance, so that if Walt ever took time to talk to her she would be able to converse with him intelligently.

After their youngest girl was married, Laura felt abandoned and useless, except when she could accompany Walt to the coast, east or west. While he took care of his business, she visited art galleries and attended matinees, sometimes evening performances, with other wives. She made one trip to Paris all on her own. She had her hair done, bought some designer clothes, took the city tours, day and night, and hated it. Seeing young lovers in embrace along the Seine, in doorways, on street corners, made her feel like an intruder. And returning to her hotel room, she felt miserably alone. She was then forty-two years old, trim and attractive; but the only man she was interested in attracting, still, was Walt, despite the fact that he had shown no interest in her—or any other woman as far as Laura knew—since her third pregnancy.

Business, it seemed to Laura, was her rival. And

as she looked around at the wives of other businessmen she got the idea that money or the pursuit of it was a common polarizer that divided the hes from the shes and kept them apart in separate magnetic circles. She was coming to suspect success and to doubt herself so much—and was so eager to talk to a man—that she consulted a psychiatrist. She was getting comfort out of therapy until the doctor told her that there was nothing really wrong with her; that, very possibly, Walt's ceaseless striving for more money and more power might be indicative of a struggle against latent homosexuality, a way to compensate for his impotence with women. This Laura resented. She regarded Walt as the most dynamic, most virile man she had ever known.

Not long afterwards Laura was rewarded with the good news that Walt was selling 83 percent of his interest in the flour mill, the doughnut bakery and the national chain of retail shops for $5 million in cash; he was also retiring from the business. Her hopes and dreams revived. Now, she told herself, with Walt as rich as he could possibly want to be, far richer than anybody else they knew, he would have time to enjoy life with her. They could move to New York, buy a town house, decorate it with art, not the most advanced, contemporary art, but anyway the modern art of their generation. And then they would travel. It would be the honeymoon they had never had and it would last for the rest of their lives.

But Walt had other plans. He had sold control of the business, he told her, because there were greater opportunities around than doughnuts. He intended to devote all his time and energies to the stock market, with the objective of doubling his $5 million in three

years. And he commenced his new career that very
evening at dinner with Elliott Hibbard, managing partner of an old St. Louis brokerage firm, who had acted
as Walt's financial adviser in the sale of his business.

For Laura the dinner was one dish of acid after
another. Although Elliott Hibbard turned out to be
a distinguished-looking bachelor, about Walt's age,
who had done all the things and been to all the
places that Laura had in mind, she hardly spoke to
him. She regarded him as an enemy who, in aiding
Walt, was committing her to a life sentence of solitary
freedom.

In bed that night Laura pushed Walt to a showdown.
She explained how she felt. And he declared how
it was going to be. She could travel if she liked.
She could have a new house to decorate any way
she pleased. He was staying put in St. Louis and
becoming an active, full-time investor. To Laura's
surprise, and no doubt to Walt's, she announced that
she was leaving him. In the morning she moved to
a hotel.

If she expected Walt to relent, Laura had miscal-
culated. As she later learned from her daughters, Walt
had become entirely absorbed in studying investment
ideas.

Although Laura had paid little attention to Elliott
Hibbard at their dinner meeting, the reverse was not
true. When he heard about the split-up, he phoned
and asked to see her. Elliott was everything that Laura
had ever wanted Walt to be—polished, cosmopolitan,
casual about his money and his power. As soon as
the law allowed, Laura divorced Walt in Mexico City
and married Elliott. On their honeymoon they circled
the globe with stopovers in the Far East, where his

cultural interest was centered. For Laura it was all very romantic, very fascinating. And yet when they returned to St. Louis, Laura was vaguely unsatisfied. Not with her marriage—oh no, Elliott was proving to be a devoted, instructive companion, and even her daughters and sons-in-law were impressed by him. It was not Elliott who left her unsatisfied but Walt.

Walt's continuing independence of her was still a nagging irritation. It gave her a little relief when Elliott invited Walt to take his brokerage business elsewhere, at her urging. But after twenty-some years together, she wanted the satisfaction of knowing that her departure was regretted, at least noticed. And then it occurred to her that in Elliott she had the perfect, divinely appointed instrument of her revenge. What did Walt want more than her? To double his money. Who knew more about making money in the market than Walt? Elliott. Although he had already made part of a million by investing, Walt was a beginner compared to Elliott, who had been at it all his life, practically. If Walt was an apt student, Elliott was an authority, the best in town, the expert adviser on whom Walt himself had relied for years.

As Laura saw it, the only weakness in her plan for having the old husband outdone by the new was that Elliott preferred to stay out of the market as an investor. "I try to retain perspective," he explained. "I don't want my personal position to influence the advice I give my clients, even subconsciously. Besides, my capital is tied up in my firm; that's where I get the greatest return on my investment."

While Laura appreciated Elliott's high-minded attitude, she wished he would compromise for her. She was convinced that because Walt was so competitive his ego would be smashed once he came out second-best. When Elliott remained adamant, Laura decided to challenge Walt to an investment contest herself. Tapping the $100,000 trust fund set up for her by Walt, she opened a brokerage account with Elliott. Her objective? To double her money before Walt doubled his, although that was not how she expressed it to her husband.

To Laura's dismay, the handling of her account was at first delegated to a house man. "I like women," Elliott was constrained once again to explain himself, "too much to do business with, maybe. Feminine emotions are very winning, but not in the stock market." Nonetheless this particular principle or prejudice of Elliott's—a not uncommon one among stockbrokers—collapsed before his wife's insistence.

Walt's approach to investing in stocks was not unlike the approach he had used to set up his chain of doughnut-and-coffee shops. He counted on people to make things happen. A shrewd judge of men, he favored self-motivated drivers like himself. And so he bought the shares of companies whose chief executives were known to crack a loud whip and whose motivation was insured by adequate stock options or holdings. As long as these men ran their companies to increase profits fast, Walt held on to his stock and bought more in market dips. He was not concerned with price, however, only with earnings. He couldn't care less whether the public bid the price up or down on a daily basis. He was patient, firmly believing that as the earnings went, so would the price of the stock in due course, and only a management that doubled earnings could double the value of his investment.

Laura, despite her certificate from the New York Institute of Finance, started out with a sentimental preference for the established names of her youth— chemical companies, steels and utilities now fully matured—whose rate of growth had long ago flattened out. But, keeping tabs on Walt's progress through their children, Laura soon began to demand comparable performance for her own portfolio. Amused by her passion for the market but as yet unaware of her underlying purpose, Elliott recommended some sound stocks in the rapid-growth, higher-risk category.

Summing up the next few years in a few sentences, Laura did very nicely in the market, which happened to be booming at the time. But Walt did even better. And when he achieved his objective of doubling his investment, Laura turned bitter toward Elliott. With all his expertise, Laura was now convinced, Elliott could never best Walt if his life depended on it. Walt had more get-up-and-go, more aggressive spirit and intensity of purpose. As he liked to say, men who fought hard to win came out ahead of those who thought hard about winning.

When she complained to Elliott about the rate of return on her investment, he told her that if she needed more money she had only to ask him for it.

Laura remained dissatisfied. Neither Elliott's attentions nor the opportunity to travel extensively was adequate compensation for her failure to "punish" Walt. More and more now, she spent her days, as Walt did, preoccupied with her investments, even using her children to ferret out Walt's holdings so that she might buy in on his winners.

Romantic aspects aside, the triangle illustrates several financial points.

Walt bought people, not stocks. Because he was a good judge of men and what made them perform at their best, his investment approach was simple and effective, especially since he stayed on top of his stocks constantly and rode with his winners, making the most of every opportunity.

Laura was doing well enough—for any reasonable investor. With all her advantages she might even have achieved her goal of surpassing Walt's performance had she learned the lesson of patience from her first husband and of objectivity from the second.

Alan, as a registered trader, had everything he needed for success: floor information, a talent for trading, experience, and knowhow. He lacked only detachment, the capacity to keep calm under pressure when the money on the line was his own.

Arnie, the C.P.A., possessed the ability to appraise securities values shrewdly. But he lacked two things— the resources to buy what he liked and the strength of character to avoid compromising his own standards of quality. He lost his cool when he found himself writing the cost of his investments in a checkbook instead of in a practice ledger.

In all three of the case records cited, the principals were plentifully supplied with good investment ideas, the seeds of market success. But just as seeds usually need fertile soil, moisture and sunlight, so investment ideas, to come to fruition, require nourishment in the form of adequate financial resources along with a compatible environment in terms of the investor's character and temperament.

16

The
Cons, the Pros
and You

Willie Sutton, the notorious bank robber, was being interviewed by the prison psychiatrist, who asked, "Willie, why do you always pick on banks?" "You jerk," replied Willie, according to the story, "that's where the money is."

The stock market also is where the money is. And robbery aside, the opportunity is there for anyone who is willing to pay the price in time and study and, if necessary, in self-discipline. Money is made and lost in carloads every day on Wall Street. While the money-makers may differ in personality, and their approaches or investment media may be poles apart, they are all similar in one respect: the way they do it is compatible with what they hope to accomplish. There is logic to their buy and sell decisions. If for some it is a game, as the latter-day "Adam Smith" contends, then it is a very rational game, more like chess than Parcheesi. With most big winners the market is a business, cause and effect, as witness the style of Bernard Baruch, probably the biggest winner in modern times. If Baruch ever felt like a player in a game it was after the close, counting the score.

There are consistent winners who try to catch an issue on the rise, so as to have their judgment preconfirmed, and others who prefer to fish along the bottoms.

There are consistent winners who follow the rule of cutting their losses fast, on the theory that "the first loss is the cheapest," and others who will patiently wait out a basically sound situation until it turns around and fulfills its promise.

Some carefully avoid "throwing good money after bad," while others, proud of having "the courage of their convictions," habitually average down.

Some, basically optimistic, are always buyers, and others, basically pessimistic, are short sellers.

What's the difference how they make money, as long as they do?

Most consistent winners are probably fundamentalists for whom the bell rings on value (high earnings: low price), but a great many are triggered by technical signs (price movement: volume) on the tape or on charts.

Some hunt out special situations, others are more comfortable riding with the fastest-growing company in the fastest-growing industry, or that which appears to be.

Some play it safe by hedging, others relish the long odds in venture capital situations.

Some believe in diversifying their portfolios, others in concentrating on a very few very strong issues.

So what?

Since all of these approaches work for some (and do not work for many others), it's not the vehicle, it's the driver. The way to choose your investment vehicle and your investment route is to suit your own style of driving. Which means that you must, first of all, have expert knowledge of the speed, durability, braking power and general performance characteristics of the individual in control, namely you. Because no matter how splendid your destination, if your market route gives you the shakes, if it seems too fast or too slow, too bumpy or too dull, if you are dizzied by the spins or too exhilarated at the heights, you may be forced to detour or even to drop out along the way.

But since for every investor style there is at least one viable, compatible investment approach, it's just as easy to suit oneself as not.

A thirty-five-year veteran of Wall Street who for most of that time has held a high-level observation post says that the most successful investor he has ever encountered is an Englishman who adheres to a simple formula. He buys stocks only when the risk-reward ratio is 1:5 or better; that is, when the upside potential is at least 50 percent within the year, and the downside risk no greater than 10 percent.

Can you stick like epoxy to a strict risk-reward ratio, ignoring all other temptations? Then take it, it's yours.

A Montreal multimillionaire adds to his fortune systematically on the American Stock Exchange by purchasing convertible bonds and converting them to common stock as soon as possible. If the stocks runs up, it is sold to buy more bonds, which in turn are promptly converted into more stock, which as it appreciates is used to buy more convertible bonds. When the market is active, so is the Montreal arbitrageur who may turn over his money a half dozen times in a good year. Of course, he arbitrages in this manner only with the more volatile issues and he must move very fast in order to catch the intra-day swings of the market. A wrinkle he likes to use is this: just before interest is due on his bonds he alerts himself to the possibility of converting as soon as the bonds have qualified for the interest. Can you stand short-term gains? Can you move as fast as the Montreal arbitrageur? If so, you are welcome to his system.

Gerald Loeb advocates that the time to buy a stock is when nobody else is interested. But just the opposite advice comes from Jesse Livermore, who also rates as an authority, having amassed and dissipated several substantial piles on Wall Street. "Experience has proved to me," declared Livermore, "that the real money made in speculating has been in commitments in a stock or commodity showing a profit right from the start."

These two distinctly contradictory opinions reflect two distinctly different personality types—the downtick and the uptick, they might be called. Both can (and do) argue their positions persuasively with statistics, charts and computer printouts. In essence, theirs is the classic controversy between the pessimist and the optimist as to whether half a glass of water is 50 percent empty or 50 percent full. The downtick personality holds that it is less risky and potentially more rewarding to buy a deeply depressed issue in anticipation of an eventual upturn. And the uptick personality maintains that while there is never a guarantee that any particular stock will move either way, the odds are improved when the arrow is already pointing in the right direction.

Since you may be right or wrong on either side of the issue, you may as well enlist in the one that conforms to your own attitude or personal style.

A Washington attorney was making money in the market at a time when most stockholders were losers. He did it through politicial sensitivity combined with logic or luck. Becoming aware, in 1968, of a rising tide of consumerism in our national life, and a growing popular concern over ecology and its natural offspring, pollution control, he heard a sell signal and a buy signal, both loud and clear. Liquidating his oil stocks, which were doing well enough at the moment, the attorney reinvested the proceeds in shares of a beer and a cosmetics company whose non-controversial products his family used and liked. It proved to be a good move. From January 2, 1969, through June 10, 1970, while the sticky oils as a group were losing 37.8 percent of market value, the cosmetics group was gaining 9.4 percent, and the brewers 14.5 percent. For the record, though, the attorney might have been served equally well had he caught a smoke signal, because during the same period the cigarette and the cigar groups also rose strongly against the heavy downdraft.

Two years out of the University of Pennsylvania, an enterprising, high-spirited young man invested all the capital he and his wife could raise, $60,000. Five years later he was worth a half million, and making progress toward the second half. He did it by using his funds as seed capital for a new company—the kind of venture in which a good many older, richer and presumably wiser men have lost their shirts. But to this particular young man the established companies, even those with a rapid rate of growth, appeared stodgy. He would not have been satisfied to double his money in five years, four years or three. He was aiming at 1,000 percent appreciation and he was willing to take 100 percent risk. Are you? Do you have enough faith in your judgment or instinct to put money on a man and his idea? (Remember, a Memorex or Teledyne just starting out will not have a record of sales and earnings, solid or otherwise.) And do you have the persistence to stay with it year after barren year while your friends may be showing 10 percent to 25 percent appreciation annually on relatively low-risk investments? If so, you need not be put off by bear or bull markets. In the former you are more apt to find attractive venture capital situations, and in the latter you are more apt to cash in by way of a new-issue offering to the public.

It has been my good fortune to know an accomplished chartist named Ed. During the 1967–68 phase of the bull market Ed's charts gave him all the right readings. When he bought a stock, it promptly found support. And when he sold a stock, it inevitably met early resistance. In 1969 and 1970 when the market fell on its face, Ed's charts gave him all the wrong readings. He still believes in his charts, however. *They* are right every time, he insists. The trouble is, he explains, that sometimes *he* is wrong in his interpretations.

A system, being something that works at least part of the time for somebody, is also something that works at least part of the time for nobody. No system can guarantee anything in the market except what the individual makes of it.

One successful investor remains fully invested at all times. Another lightens up on his securities and converts to cash in uncertain markets. The first prunes his weak holdings and adds to the strong. The second uses his liquidity to pick up good values when the market shows a definite trend. Who is right or who is wrong depends on who makes the most of his method.

A very able broker named Victor, who works in a Madison Avenue boardroom was visited one day by the president of an up-and-coming computer programming company, who said that he had been referred to Victor by one of his good clients. The visitor—lets call him Henry—opened a discretionary account, declaring that he didn't care if he took long- or short-term gains or losses and that he would give Victor just six months to prove himself.

At no time did Henry interfere with the handling of his account, or even ask questions. At the end of six months when his equity had been increased by 30 percent, Henry paid a call on his broker. Displaying a computer printout detailing every single buy and sell in his account over the six-month period, Henry wanted to know Victor's winning system. And when Victor could not tell him, Henry became nervous. The printout suggested, prompted Henry, that the broker was exceptionally consistent on the buys but rather random on the sells. What about that? Victor couldn't say.

Disappointed, Henry closed out his account. Unless he could isolate the specific areas of judgment by which his broker had done so well for him—and 30 percent appreciation in six months, he acknowledged, was the best performance he had ever achieved—he could feel no confidence in the future. Since Victor could find no trace of pattern in his own actions, they struck Henry as hit or miss, like pinning the tail on the donkey while blindfolded. Despite proof to the tune of 30 percent capital appreciation, Henry was more comfortable entrusting his investments to a broker who had a system that could be either validated or criticized.

Eccentric as Henry might seem, he represents a fairly common type.

Or, as Victor expressed it: "There is something to Henry's insistence that his broker or investment adviser be consistent, because I find that the people who make the most money in the market year after year are those who do indeed have a system—although it isn't the very same one in each case.

"Just as stupid investors make the same mistakes each time, smart investors make the same smart moves each time.

"I think it is perfectly possible to make profits by always buying, never selling. It is also perfectly feasible to make profits by selling only those stocks that go down 10 percent from any level. I think it is perfectly possible to make profits by being a good technical analyst or strictly a good fundamentalist.

"Even though each one of these approaches may contradict the other, consistency may make any method profitable. That is, a trader would hardly be moving in and out of Brooklyn Union Gas, but someone who pays attention to the money market on a long-term basis could make profits by buying and selling utilities over a long period of time, provided he *consistently* applies the same criteria."

17

The Aim
and the Aimer

If there are dozens of systems that work sometimes for somebody and hundreds of thousands of individual approaches that are working out for one or more investors, let alone tens of thousands of securities to choose among, which is the way to go? What system or style or program can help fulfill your investment objectives and at the same time give you a sense of fulfillment?

Even to pick or ponder you must consider the self-evident: Before you can hope to reach your investment objective, you've got to have one; and even before you can arrive at that stage, you've got to know something about yourself—at the minimum, what you want as well as what you need.

It should be easy but it isn't. As part of a survey completed in 1969 by McKinsey & Co. for a nationwide brokerage house, a sampling of clients, about 50,000, was queried as to "reason for investing." The response indicated that the overwhelming majority, better than 80 percent, were in the market for either "capital gains" or a "hedge against inflation."

Sensible, practical reasons—beat the tax system or beat the deterioration of the dollar. But are these good reasons the real reasons?

If most investors really meant to blunt the bite of the I.R.S., wouldn't it be logical to assume that they would be purchasing securities with appreciation potential over the intermediate to long term and, therefore, should not be evaluating the results of their actions for at least six months? Or, if most investors meant merely to take enough money out of the market to keep a few percentage points ahead of the persistent-and-steepening decline in the purchasing power of their dollars, wouldn't it be logical to assume that they would be holding securities which yielded 5 percent or better and offered some prospect of moderate earnings growth, without much risk?

But, significantly, only a minority of those whose stated objective is "capital gains" or a "hedge against inflation" act as we assume they should. They give the right answers for the wrong actions. While their ostensible aim in the market is financial, their performance tends to be emotional. Undoubtedly, they need what they say they do. And presumably they want what they say they need. But then personality takes over. They are tempted to adventure. They compete and try to beat. They hope to prove or to vindicate themselves. They adjust their program not to keep up with changing market or economic conditions but with friends and neighbors. Some of them find a route to failure and follow it doggedly to the dead end.

Although we regard the stock market objectively as a place to make money, most of us purchase more than profit potential or dividend income with our stock. Whether we know it or not, we are bidding for happiness, for power, for achievement, for a feeling of security, prestige, an outlet for our frustrations in business or marriage, challenge, an opportunity to try our skills against fairly favorable odds, a financial moon shot, or just a grown-up game that almost anybody can play. And if these are ulterior motives, so what? We all have one or more. They add to the satisfaction of success. There's nothing wrong with ulterior motives, as such, as long as they don't get in the way and each investor clearly recognizes his own. Otherwise, there may be ambivalent objectives, contrary purposes, and a penalty to pay.

Often more costly than the motive that is unrecognized or vague is the clear, logical, unambiguous aim that is negated by the method or follow-through. Mind and emotions may be incompatible or the capacity of one may be greater than that of the other. Let's say the man wants capital gains and that, indeed, is what he needs. He's picked a promising portfolio of stocks for that purpose. He has nothing to do now but keep an eye on his holdings. But the market is uncertain and the man is nervous. He gets clammy palms when the price of one of his stocks fluctuates downward. He hears and reads about other stocks, owned by other people, that are going up faster and straighter than his. He endures his fears and doubts as long as he can and then sells on an interim rise or fall of a few points. A long-term goal, yes, with a short-term fuse.

Fear, impatience, lapse of objectivity—these are the common enemies of the investor who may know his own mind but has yet to become thoroughly acquainted with the state of his heart. Many a man of means has missed the opportunity to multiply his capital, simply because he could not bring himself to risk his money in any investment whose yield was less than the savings bank rate of interest.

And there really is no point in making an investment —no matter how logical financially—with which the investor cannot live.

A healthy exercise for anyone in the market is to investigate himself regularly by posing some basic questions, such as:

Why am I risking my money?

And for what other reason besides profits or income?

Exactly what are my financial goals—expressed in dollars or percentages?

And what are my nonfinancial goals?

Can I be happy with the attainment of my goals if others—motivated by similar or different needs—seem to be doing better than I? In other words, how self-sufficient am I? How competitive?

Will I be satisfied to attain my goals—and even to surpass all others of my acquaintance—if I alone know about it? Or must I also receive the bonus of recognition or admiration or envy to feel fulfilled?

In short: What am I doing here? And how high is up for me?

The successful investor usually knows what he hopes to accomplish, and selects his investments accordingly.

A case in point is Gene. While he makes no big gains in the market, Gene suffers no great losses, either. He is sixty-four. "At my age," he says comfortably, "I don't want to make all the money in the world, I just want to hold on to what I have and maybe earn 10 percent a year in appreciation plus dividends." Gene gets what he wants, primarily with utilities shares.

There are many Genes, near or in retirement, who are less concerned with profits than with preserving principal plus earning enough of a dividend to offset inflation and top the interest rate of savings banks.

There are also many 10-share buyers who will never make much of a killing on Wall Street but who really aren't in it for big money. Maybe they just want to be part of the crowd or near the action. Maybe they're looking for prudent participation in a common experience, to show their faith in country or company or in themselves. Maybe they can't afford more than the cost of 10 shares. In any case, many an odd-lot buyer, the supposedly always-wrong "little man," is satisfied to make a socio-religio-ego commitment with less to gain financially than psychologically.

State of mind produces more than individual profits and losses. When shared by enough investors, it can cause the market indicators to point up or down, and has even been known to provide the impetus for boom or bust. The bull market of 1967–68 died from economic, business and political ailments, to be sure. But the great bear market of 1969–70, the longest, sharpest decline since whenever, was kept alive and kicking by the irrational selling of hundreds of professional money managers as well as of hundreds of thousands of shareholders—a manifestation characterized as "a kind of neurosis" by George P. Schultz, then secretary of Labor.

Since rational investment judgment is more apt to grow out of sensible aims, it may be useful to look over the four main classifications employed by stock analysts to aid investors in gauging the appropriateness of selected issues. Although securities classifications vary somewhat among brokerage houses and investment advisers, as a rule they all take into account three organic elements: investor temperament; the balance between risk and potential reward; and time.

1. *Low risk with high return.* For the conservative investor who requires above-average quality for safety of principal with yields of 4 to 5 percent and moderate growth potential of 3 to 5 percent, or about enough to offset the upward trend in the cost of living. The investor who holds stocks in this category is usually expecting a secure return from dividends and per-share earnings growth combined of 8 to 10 percent a year.

2. *Consistent growth.* For the long-term investor who seeks relatively steady growth in per-share earnings at a rate faster than that of the general economy, plus moderate current yield, or a combined return from basic growth and dividends of 10 to 15 percent. The downside risk may be about 10 percent and the upside potential about 30 percent—over a period of six months to two years.

3. *Moderate risk performance.* For the value-conscious investor with the temperament to go against the current market vogue, who is willing and able to wait from six to eighteen months generally for unusual profit opportunities to develop out of potential turnaround situations or overlooked growth issues. The risk-reward ratio may be in the neighborhood of 15:45.

4. *Higher risk performance.* For the adventurous investor who is prepared to assume considerable short-term market risk in order to participate in situations

that appear to possess exceptional appreciation potential over a period of three months to a year. The higher
risk associated with such issues may result from various
factors—high price volatility or a high price-earnings
multiple or an unpredictable earnings pattern or the
possibility of a sharp shift in market interest. The risk-
reward range may be in the area of 20:60.

Once the investor knows what he's aiming at and is
reasonably confident of being able to live with the risks
and time elements involved, he can give thought to his
market personality, which, in the final analysis, must
determine the results he achieves.

What makes for winning performance in the market?
The question was put to Harry Edelstein, a stockbroker
with excellent credentials. A psychology major at Notre
Dame and an outstanding securities salesman while
still in his twenties, Harry credits his own phenomenally
rapid success to a knack for selecting clients who had
what it took in the way of mental and emotional resources to be winners. How did he recognize his potential winners? What were the attributes that he
looked for? This is Harry's profile of a winner:

"The winner has definite and distinctive personality
traits lacking in the investor who does not do as well.

"Although there is no direct relationship between
success in the stock market and success in other fields
(*i.e.*, a trucking tycoon may do less well in the market
than one of his shipping clerks), the two sometimes go
together—in the same way that a golden retriever may
be an excellent hunting dog but a poor pet or a poor
hunting dog and a good pet or fine all around or a
complete disappointment. There are, however, certain
traits that are generally present in a successful investor.

"1. The big winner has the ability to be objective. He can look at financial data without superimposing his own subjective self. For example, he may love to bowl, but in analyzing Brunswick he does not allow his enthusiasm for the sport to affect his investment decision. Where the average investor concentrates on what stock to *buy*, the winner type looks at the picture through a broader scope, visualizing to some degree when and at what price he will be prepared to *sell*. In other words, he starts with a financial objective that he expects the stock to attain for him.

"2. The consistent winner is interested in results rather than in technique. He is interested in winning and making money over and above everything else; and he will alter—or not alter—his approach solely for the purpose of getting maximum performance.

"3. The winner has a passion for facts—relevant facts—and is not interested in rumor or unfounded opinion. He also seems to have the ability to strip shadow from substance and, as a result, to come to more substantive conclusions.

"4. Although he may change his mind, he is intrinsically a tough decision maker. By this I mean he pushes all gray areas into either black or white areas, enabling him to view things more clearly. When he is unable to do this, he may back off until it can be done.

"5. He seems to have what I call *feel*. However, feel is a very poor word since it implies an element of luck. O. J. Simpson, Joe Namath and Willie Mays all have feel. It may be indefinable but it's as real and evident in the winner as any other of his qualities. Because it is difficult to define does not make it less real.

"6. He is highly individualistic. Just as there are

many ways to win a football game, there are also many ways to win in the stock market.

"7. The winner has great intestinal fortitude. Bad news does not scare him off but, rather, is weighed in the context of his entire investment philosophy; and, if the news can be taken advantage of in any way, he will take advantage of it. Similarly, if a stock has had a run-up, it is not necessarily viewed as a sell, because he is not afraid to hold if he feels the issue can continue to go higher.

"8. The winner seems to view his investments as a business. He knows he will have to take losses and he knows that taking a loss is inevitable.

"9. He does not over-react emotionally to stimulus. Where the average investor may buy or sell on financial news, the winner will view the situation in perspective and may even go against the grain if he thinks the market reaction is lopsided.

"10. He is persistent. He will hammer away until he succeeds. He does not discourage easily and he is confident that he will eventually be exactly what he is becoming; *i.e.*, a winner.

"11. He is realistic. By this I mean he seems to be mature in his judgments and does not expect miracles. He does not look back on his bad decisions or waste time fretting about his mistakes.

"12. He thinks big. This applies to quality as well as quantity. His mind is not cluttered with trivia, and he expects bigger results than does the average investor.

"13. He is positive. Though he pretty much sees things as they are, he is nevertheless optimistic about the future.

"14. Character determines success or failure. In the

case of a winner, the results of his investments seem to arrange themselves in the image and pattern of his personality so that in the end he receives—as does everyone in the stock market—the success or failure he deserves."

If you can claim Harry's fourteen winning attributes for yourself, congratulations, you've got it made!

But if you can't, should you liquidate your holdings and steer clear of the market? Or resign yourself to being merely *average?*

Perhaps.

Or, since success and failure are both largely a matter of habit, why not cultivate the habit of success?

Or—as do some investors who recognize their failings but who can't or won't do anything about it—select a broker or investment adviser with the understanding, concern and vitality to act as your equilibrator, to be crutch or spur, father image or whipping boy, whatever may be needed to balance off your shortcomings and, so, to strip the subjective from the objective in the critical decision-making process.

Or—as do some investors who have lost all confidence in themselves—give yourself a *grand illusion* by empowering another to assume discretion for your market decisions, thus ridding yourself of responsibility for failure and reserving to yourself full credit for success.

"No investor is hopeless," declares an experienced broker whose clientele seem to bear out his words. "Regardless of quirks or idiosyncrasies or weaknesses, there is lots of hope for anyone who will take the trouble to evaluate for himself his investment performance by some objective method.

"I find that the best way to evaluate performance is

simply to watch the equity in the account—that is, to disregard whether any one particular stock has been sold at a gain or a loss. If there is a general upward trend in the equity of the portfolio, the 6-point loss in any one stock doesn't matter. What the investor really wants is to be *worth more*. And even if the investor merely wants ego gratification, I find he can be trained to be ego-gratified by an increase in his net worth—which is all he should logically be interested in anyway.

"Thus, if I have 10 stocks and sell 9 of them at a loss of 2 points in each, I wouldn't be too unhappy if the tenth went up 100 percent. Men have made millions losing a little on 9 stocks and hitting it big on the tenth.

"This approach would eliminate the constant confidence-eroding soul-searching about what should have been held and what should have been sold. If the equity of the portfolio can show constant increase regardless of so-called mistakes, the investor will end up being a big success. This approach would also help the investor get out of the bad habit of focusing all his attention on individual transactions instead of on the full results of his investment program, where it should be."

18

The
Investor's Mirror

You look into a mirror and see something askew. What do you do?

Whatever you can, probably.

If this book has served its purpose thus far it has provided a kind of investor's mirror, holding up to the light of inquiry examples of distinctive market personalities in order to enable you to catch reflections of yourself in style or in action, in shadow or in portrait. Now what's to be done about it?

Bernard Baruch, who took a dim view of the usefulness of advice, unless addressed to "those who are able to muster the necessary self-discipline," expressed an interesting attitude toward the "instructive effect" of examples:

"Other people's mistakes, I have noticed, often make

us only more eager to try to do the same thing. Perhaps it is because in the breast of every man there burns not only that divine spark of discontent but the urge to 'beat the game' and show himself smarter than the other fellow. In any case, *only after we have repeated these errors for ourselves does their instructive effect sink home.*"

Until about the time Baruch was born, anyone confronted with his own imperfections might have been expected to respond fatalistically: we are what we are and the leopard cannot change his spots, etc. But it is no longer the custom for a rational man merely to take comfort from his revealed strengths and to resign himself to his failings. Thanks to Sigmund Freud, who, by taking a deep look into himself, without precedent or counselor to guide him, was able to free his latent creative powers and, in consequence, to establish for the first time precedent, theory and cadre for several schools of counselors. Half a century after Freud demonstrated that self-knowledge could be more than self-indulgence or morbid introspection, that it could lead directly to self-improvement, in 1942 to be precise, Karen Horney produced her popular book, *Self-Analysis,* extending the precedent and the theory by means of case histories. Nongeniuses also, it seemed, could practice self-analysis and profit from it.

While we are not concerned here with psychotherapy, the background is pertinent to the premise that our adult personalities are not set in concrete. With intelligent effort, acquired traits can be shed and habit patterns can be restructured.

The Russians, who reject Freudianism and psychoanalysis as we know it, regard personality as a collection of conditioned reflexes. Inspired initially by Pavlov's famous experiments with dogs, the Russian therapists hold that conditioned reflexes can be reconditioned, in effect ignoring the cause and treating the symptom. In our own country, a related thesis has been argued by Andrew Salter's *Conditioned Reflex Therapy*, published in 1949. Followers of this approach believe it is not even necessary to expose root causes in order to eliminate undesirable characteristics and to replace them with more desirable ones. Rehabituation is the key.

So much for the sick psyche. We are interested in whether the functioning but less-than-fully-effective investor can alter his market personality in such a manner as to upgrade his profit performance.

Bernard Baruch, we know, did just that. By and for himself. As a new investor, he made mistakes and lost money. Wishing to learn why, in order that he might try to do better, he examined his methods in the light of their consequences. He found patterns of behavior that he could relate to mistakes and losses. He determined to break those habits that were counterproductive. And he did, substituting new habits that were calculated to work better for him. A self-perfectionist, Baruch examined himself regularly to improve his market style. As a result, he turned out to be one of the most spectacularly successful investor-speculators in the history of the stock market. In his autobiography, he stresses the importance of constant self-analysis and self-adjustment.

Do I hear, "Well, Baruch may be the exception that proves the rule; the fact that he did it that way doesn't mean anyone else can"?

True, too true, alas, as to degree of success. Times and tax rates have changed. But the principle is still as valid as ever. To the measure of our own capacities and within the limits of the capital gains statutes, what Baruch did to improve himself you can do and so can I. I know that to be a fact, because I have done it— although in a modest way—and am still doing it. For me it has meant the difference between average and above-average results.

Over a dozen years ago, before I had read Baruch's remarkable book or become associated with the securities business, I began to question my investment progress. When I could not longer be appeased by the usual rationalizations—blaming poor ideas, bad timing, rotten executions, and so on—I started to compare my market record with that of others who were utilizing similar facilities and services. What I learned was not only unflattering to me but also challenging. My wife, as it happened, maintained a separate account. Sharing "my" research recommendations for ideas and "my" broker for advice and executions, and bankrolled by an even split of our investable funds, she had been making more money than I—about 10 percent a year more! It was this kind of evidence, too disturbing to accept readily and yet incontrovertible, that made me review what I was doing, how, and why. It took time and an uncomfortable exercise in humility, but I found a pattern of reflexes or instincts that ended up too often in smaller profits and larger losses than seemed necessary in retrospect. I had bad habits—as they might say in a TV commercial—nothing serious, just serious enough to cost me 10 percent a year!

Once identified, the culprit habits proved amenable to reform. Most of them. Some I must still cope with. At any rate, the direct consequence of my self-tinkering

was markedly improved, more consistent performance.
An indirect result is this book. For nearly all the investor weaknesses catalogued in these pages I first
came to know in myself. It was not until several years
later, after I had joined the financial community as a
working member, that I realized how many other investors—including those with basically sound programs
and suitable portfolios of securities—were handicap-
ping themselves because of personality traits at odds
with their investment aims. The most common and
costly mistakes I encountered were these:

Holding on to a failing stock just to get even
Trying to strike it rich too fast
Acting on rumors, say-so or insider tips
Striving always to buy at the low and sell at the high
Going for price rather than value—or confusing the
two
Blindly tagging along after friends and associates
Investing in emotional spasms, sometimes rash,
sometimes overly deliberate
Allowing fear or timidity to negate hard facts and
common sense
Relying completely on technical research and ignor-
ing the fundamentals
Buying stocks as if they were lottery tickets, without
considering the odds, or risk-reward ratio
Using sophisticated techniques inappropriately, us-
ually for social status or prestige
Refusing to accept a loss or responsibility for a loss
Impatience: buying and selling just to keep in action
Hedging indiscriminately
Losing objectivity under pressure
And worst of all, not learning from mistakes.

All common or costly habits are not bad habits, of course.

If, for instance, you are distracted from current opportunities by misgivings over something you have already sold out of, only you can decide whether the self-pity or self-loathing thus permitted you is worth the price you're paying.

Or, possibly, you may be one of those demanding souls who feels he must not only be right, he must be *absolutely* right. You have bought a stock at 20 and it goes to 40½. Do you find that you cannot bring yourself to sell the stock after it dips to 38½, just because it was once two points higher? After you have determined which is basically more rewarding to you, the supreme triumph of being absolutely right or the profit of 18½ points, you may know something valuable about yourself and it should come in handy the next time you face the prospect of being *merely* right.

Or, reversing the coin, do you usually feel that the course of action you have undertaken is the wrong one? You have sold a stock at 30—at a 10-point profit— and subsequently it goes to 40. Do you immediately kick yourself and say, "I was wrong to sell the stock at 30"? Is being "wrong" an inexcusable error that impairs your self-esteem? You can have your choice— whichever means more to you: an immediate profit and the chance to kick yourself afterward, or inertia and the chance to kick yourself afterward.

Which annoys you more, losing (or making less) money on your own decision or on your broker's recommendation? When you have your answer, look around at the other investors of your acquaintance. Are any of them buying at the bottoms and selling at the tops? This just can't be done, as Bernard Baruch has put it, "except by liars."

Does it please you to be known as "a man with a broker"? Do you enjoy having an audience when you give orders to your broker? And, carried away by it all, do you place orders you later regret? If so, after computing the cost of "establishing" yourself, you may very well start to concentrate on the joys of making money.

Do you disregard the risks of investing? Do you pretend that you are in on a sure thing? Is the "good broker" for you one who encourages your hopes? Is what you want to hear "the market's fine, it's going up" or "we've done just the right thing"? Euphoria comes high. It's much more economical—though worrisome—to acknowledge the risks involved.

Money is not everything in the market either, however. If your peccadilloes give you pleasure or satisfaction and if you can afford to pay for them, why not? The stock market is one of the most engrossing entertainments available in an advanced society—competitive, active and various, accessible during business hours, risky, and potentially rewarding even for amateurs.

For the profit-minded investor, however, the emotional considerations, while always present, are subordinated.

Let's say you have a pretty good idea of who you are or, at least, who you hope to be. If your wants and your needs coincide, your investment goal is clear. If not, you should be prepared to recognize both aspects of your "split personality" by aiming at dual objectives, such as 75 percent serious-financial and 25 percent wish-fulfillment-frivolous. Once you have selected a portfolio of securities appropriate to your particular objectives, the science of investing suddenly gives way to the art. No matter how carefully and wisely you may have chosen your issues, now your personality—and all the traits and habits that combine to make it up—exerts a critical influence on the *degree* of your success or your failure. Your patterns of spirit and of mind—generosity, greed, poise, impulsiveness, timidity, boldness, or whatever—will be affirmed over and over, at a price. But knowing yourself, having identified your life style, you should be able to temper or modify it, if necessary, to achieve the desired results.

Hopefully, measuring your performance by growth of equity, you will be able to regard yourself as eminently successful. But more than likely you will place yourself among the limited successes or, possibly, among the moderate failures. Sometimes there is something almost deliberate about limited or moderate performance, a kind of diffidence, as if the investor did not dare expect too much for fear of disappointing himself too badly. In the generally upward-trending markets we've been seeing for the past decade—with intermittent breaks every third year or so—it seems to require an effort, conscious or subconscious, not to attain reasonable objectives over the long term.

No stocks, not even the truest blue of the blue chips, offer an automatic ticket to profits. Systems and techniques for buying and selling are often little more than psychological braces, the Wall Street equivalents of Rumpelstiltskin, adopted by investors and speculators who need to feel infallible when faced with tough decisions. But stock pedigrees, brokers' assurances, formulas and mechanics notwithstanding, the investor gives the order to buy, sell, hold or pass, and, in the final analysis, it is by his decision-making personality that he

earns his profits and his losses. In short, with all the
assistance you can muster, it's always up to you!

But before you rush into a séance with yourself, a
note of caution. Self-probing can hold a peculiar, often
fatal, fascination for certain types of men and women.
After seeing themselves in the psychological nude, sus-
ceptible self-probers like to do it again and again, not
for the need of it so much as for the fun of it. Confirmed self-probers may become too preoccupied with
themselves to bother about any investment decisions.

There is a difference, obviously, between using self-
knowledge as the means to an end and using it as an
end in itself. The investor who knows himself possesses
a potential advantage in arriving at a decision. The investor who continues to contemplate himself has found
an absorbing way to defer a decision.

One's tolerance for self-probing—or the dividing line
between the contemplative and the practical—may be
deduced from certain attitudes. While the contemplative person may get a big charge out of seeing his
judgment vindicated, the practical one doesn't care
whose judgment it is, or how correct, as long as it
proves profitable. Where the contemplative may get almost as much gratification out of an idea that pans out
even if he didn't have money on it, the practical isn't
interested in academic triumph or in bearing witness to
someone else's profitable investment. While the contemplative measures himself against himself (because
if he is striving for anything it is essentially for self-
development), the practical rates his progress in dollars
and percentages.

Another, milder caution: Not everyone can or wants
to analyze himself. Not everyone could stand to see
himself stripped of his defenses. Not everyone cares to

look into a mirror—even for the admirable purpose of possible self-improvement.

For those who are shy of self-revelation, a discerning broker or investment adviser can sometimes act as a psychological counterweight, lending constructive qualities lacking in the client. On the other hand, the direct approach of offering corrective counsel, however tactful, rarely works. For instance, an investor habituated to placing price limits on his orders may not take it kindly when reminded that out of the last six buy orders at a limit the three that "got away" continued to go up and the three obtained at the specified price continued to go down.

Oddly enough, the broker who tends to see himself as a businessman or professional—cool, detached, informed—views very few investors as businessmen in the market. A few appear as happy-go-lucky transients—too much hope, too little fear—here today but probably gone tomorrow. Many resemble bank depositors, more fearful than hopeful, content to earn less and sleep more. Also, it is a rare broker who does not place himself in the center of his own particular solar system, sending his customers into orbit around him as very dependent planets.

The self-centered view is characteristic of most, broker and investor alike. The market is as we see it, often a reflection of or a projection from the way we see ourselves. Despite the superabundance of securities and the variety of systems and techniques, the razzle-dazzle of electronic communications, and the mumbo jumbo of the analytical headmen, we tend to reduce the stock market to the size of our own portfolio. Since none of us owns the 30 Dow-Jones Industrials, much less the 425 Standard and Poor's, we concentrate not on the popular indicators but on our own half dozen to two dozen holdings. In fact, one reason for the steadily increasing share-ownership in the country (over a million new investors every year) is the element of personal involvement. For imaginative people, the market presents an invitation to innovate. For conservatives, there is the appeal of tradition and orderly process. For individualists, an opportunity to buy what they please and when, to run with the crowd or counter to it, to follow their own dictates with their own money.

According to our friendly neighborhood psychiatrist, there are four basic motivations for striving to make money in the market or out of it:

1. To outdo one's father (or mother).

2. Sexual—that is, to overcome suspicion of homosexuality, or to compensate for impotence with women, by asserting dominance over men.

3. Exhibitionism—to win admiration and envy.

4. As a phase of the struggle between mature reason and adolescent narcissism—between one's main purpose and a vestigial secondary.

Lest any of the foregoing be construed as asserting that all investors are nuts—parent-contesting, homosexual, exhibitionist, befuddled by carried-over childhood fantasies—let us acknowlege that men and women in the stock market manifest the very same traits of personality as people. They invest their money in securities as they might in any other risky, potentially rewarding enterprise. They win and lose with much the same grace or lack of it that they reveal in business, sports, or romantic pursuits. Whether he does or doesn't make the most of his opportunities, the individual's market personality is not an isolated phenomenon but an integral part of his life style.

Witness the Passivist, who, if not the most conspicuous, must surely be the most afflicted type during a long bear market. Watching in fascination and horror as his holdings shrink in value month after month, he can do nothing but rationalize: "It's too late to sell and too early to buy."

Meanwhile, the Positivist makes every effort to reduce his suffering and his losses by frequently comparing his list of battered stocks against likely substitutions that are selling at lower price/earnings ratios and that offer either higher growth rates or higher dividend yields. He feels better doing something even if it is only to establish tax losses.

If it's not all objective and financial, it's not all subjective and personality projection, either, but something of both. The thinking man feels and the emotional man reasons. The market may be described as an arena of anonymously competing forces where the winners pay a tax and the losers receive a tax deduction; but in the deepest sense, success equates with fulfillment and failure with disappointment.

As we have seen, there are at least three ways to get to know yourself better so as to achieve better investment results: analyzing yourself, finding a broker or adviser who will either point out or compensate for your shortcomings, and learning by the example of others. It is to the latter approach, necessarily, that this book has been devoted.

Of course, if you are satisfied with your performance, leave well enough alone. Or, if you're not entirely satisfied but don't mind paying a bit extra for an emotional outlet, more power to you. As long as you know what you're doing, and the price, you are way ahead of most investors. But if you wish to raise your IQ—Investment Quotient—recognizing your market personality should help you modify it to suit your investment objectives.

As Tennyson put it:

Self-reverence, self-knowledge, self-control,—
These three alone lead life to sovereign power.